THE VAASTU WORKBOOK

THE VAASTU WORKBOOK

USING THE SUBTLE ENERGIES OF THE INDIAN ART OF PLACEMENT TO ENHANCE HEALTH, PROSPERITY, AND HAPPINESS IN YOUR HOME

TALAVANE KRISHNA, M.D.

Destiny Books
Rochester, Vermont

Destiny Books
One Park Street
Rochester, Vermont 05767
www.InnerTraditions.com

Destiny Books is a division of Inner Traditions International

Library of Congress Cataloging-in-Publication Data
Krishna, Talavane.
The vaastu workbook : using the subtle energies of the Indian art of placement to enhance health, prosperity, and happiness in your home / Talavane Krishna.
p. cm.
Includes bibliographical references.
ISBN 0-89281-940-5
1. Vaastu. I. Title.
BF1779.V38 K75 2001
133.3'33—dc21
2001002777

Printed and bound in Canada

Text design by Virginia L. Scott Bowman
This book was typeset using Life with Felix Titling as the display typeface

To all the sages who gave us the vedic wisdom of vaastu, which guides us to live harmoniously with the universe; to Mr. Geretta Reddy, whose vast experience and knowledge taught me many subtle aspects of vaastu science; and most of all to my spiritual master, Sri Ranga.

CONTENTS

ACKNOWLEDGMENTS

I WOULD LIKE TO ACKNOWLEDGE and thank the many people who helped and guided me in the completion of this book. Foremost among them are my wife, Anita, and my friend and publisher, Ehud C. Sperling. Many thanks for the infinite patience of Jon Graham and Jeanie Levitan, the editorial staff at Destiny Books. I also am grateful to my friends Kris Kilham and Sahana and many other Western friends who encouraged me to write this book.

INDUS VALLEY FOUNDATION

THE INDUS VALLEY FOUNDATION (IVF) is a nonprofit organization in Mysore, Karnataka State, India, aimed at promoting ayurveda worldwide. IVF—under the name of Indus Valley Ayurvedic Center (IVAC)—conducts many activities including Panchakarma and Rejuvenation therapies, research in ayurveda, formulation of herbal products, yoga, and meditation. IVAC also has a very active educational program, including comprehensive training for ayurvedic therapists and nutritionists, short courses in ayurveda designed especially for people from overseas, and month-long courses on ayurvedic pulse diagnosis and vaastu.

Dr. Talavane Krishna directs the IVAC program with a team of experts in various aspects of ayurveda and related vedic sciences. IVAC is situated on fifteen beautiful acres of perfect vaastu land filled with coconut palms and various tropical flowering trees and plants. All the structures were built and arranged in accordance with vaastu tenets. The center's eight-acre herb garden is one of the finest in the country, with more than eight hundred species of medicinal plants arranged according to vaastu and astrological specifications. Visitors are welcome at the center in Mysore or via the Web at www.ayurindus.com. Vaastu Consultation Services are available at the center and through the website. IVAC can also be contacted through e-mail: ivac@canada.com.

MY PERSONAL STORY

SINCE EARLY CHILDHOOD I have been very inquisitive. I wanted to know about everything around me and why things were the way they were. In school I first became fascinated with physics because it answered many of my questions. Later I studied Western medicine in India and continued my postgraduate work in the U.K. and Canada. After this I practiced medicine in the United States for sixteen years.

The twists and turns of life brought me back to my homeland of India in October 1994. My family and I moved into a house that had been under construction for more than six years. Unbeknownst to us, it had several vaastu defects. Soon the trouble started. Health and financial problems began mounting. The construction costs on the house were rising beyond our means. Accidents occurred frequently in the house. The members of my family seemed to be constantly ill, though in most cases no specific disease could be diagnosed. My wife Anita—who had begun to suffer from unexplained fevers—became totally bedridden for six weeks because of a slipped disk. Then our house contractor died suddenly of a heart attack. Several months later our electrical contractor also died of a heart attack. It seemed as though anything that could go wrong did, and even things that should have gone smoothly somehow found a way to go wrong as well.

Some friends who visited our house and saw our plight recommended that we seek the guidance of a consultant in vaastu, the vedic science of architecture and household harmony. This we did, turning to Geretta Reddy—a highly respected vaastu consultant—for advice.

While I had never practiced vaastu, from the time I was ten I had been exposed to ayurveda, the Indian system of medicine that has a history of several thousand years to its credit. Ayurveda and vaastu, both being vedic sciences, share many basic principles. Ayurveda is based on an entirely different philosophy from that of Western medicine, one that considers the body and mind as integral parts of a holistic system of living. Thus, ayurveda practitioners believe that in treating a disease one should consider the mind and body as a single unit. The influence of the planets and the five basic elements—ether, air, fire, water, and earth—are all taken into consideration while diagnosing a health problem.

Along with practicing Western medicine, I had begun to seriously study this ancient health system. The more I learned, the more my fascination with it increased. Its scientifc approach to holistic living, which takes all aspects of the life force into consideration, was extremely appealing to me. The new insights provided by the study of this ancient science were in direct contrast to Western medicine, but because ayurveda was successful in curing my own health problems—when Western medicine had not been—I knew there was something to it.

While studying ayurvedic pulse diagnosis, I also noted a consistent pattern in the interrelationship between the five basic elements and the planetary forces. I found that the interplay between them was the key to all happenings in life, and everything in the world had a direct or indirect relationship that could be traced to these forces. I began to see the connections between the three vedic sciences—ayurveda, vaastu, and jyotish, vedic astrology. So I had arrived at a point in my life where my own experience had convinced me of the valid basis of traditional Indian knowledge and, considering the plague of troubles affecting our household, I was ready to embrace vaastu if it would help.

When Mr. Reddy came to the house, he told us of our past history of unfortunate events before any of us had given him a single detail about our situation. He quickly identified all the vaastu defects of our property and revealed how our problems were related to these defects. He showed great compassion and took a genuine interest in our situation. With his motivation and guidance we corrected the vaastu. His most important advice was to remove the front entrance door and close it with a permanent wall. Amazingly enough, my wife became completely cured of her slipped disk twenty-four hours after we repaired this defect. In addition, her fevers disappeared. This was a decisive moment for us, and we soon corrected most of the other defects to put ourselves back on the right track.

Vaastu's effects are sometimes subtle, but at other times they can be astonishingly direct. For example, I decided that I wanted to buy the property that bordered mine to the North. Unfortunately, the owners already had an agreement with another party and had received twenty-five percent of the sale price as a down payment from them. It was a solid deal and I believed that my chances of buying the property were zero.

I mentioned my desire to buy the neighboring property to Mr. Reddy and jokingly asked whether I would be able to purchase the property if I changed our property's vaastu according to his recommendations. He looked straight into my eyes and said, "Yes, you will get that property. If I am wrong, I will buy twenty-five acres of land and give it to you myself." When I asked Mr. Reddy how he could be so sure, he smiled and said, "Vaastu is not a superficial thing. It requires a lot of sensitive and intuitive knowledge." He told me that he had noted the time when I asked the question and observed the direction in which I was standing and he had taken these things into consideration before he answered. Soon I made the vaastu changes he had recommended, which were to correct some defects related to a wood-burning water heater in the Northeast part of the house.

A few days after making the corrections I received a call from my neighbor, who told me the first buyer had reneged on his commitment. He asked if I was still interested in the property. I jumped at the offer and bought it right away.

At the time, a large sum of our money had been tied up for many months in a legal battle, and this was creating a financial drain. The fence on the North side of our property was practically touching the house, while there was much more space between the house and the fence on the South side. According to vaastu, this causes financial choking. As soon as I bought the property next door, I removed the fence. The very next day the message came that the legal battle was over, and I received my money soon after.

Anita and I decided to intensify our study of vaastu, and Mr. Reddy generously extended himself to teach us. Following his advice, we planned and built a correct vaastu house ourselves, choosing a location recommended by Mr. Reddy. We have been living in that new house since August 1998. In contrast to the house we had originally moved into, our new house has given us nothing but peace and contentment.

For the past four years we have studied the vaastu of many dwellings and found a perfect correlation between the lives of the inhabitants and the vaastu of their homes. We have also designed several vaastu homes for family members and friends, who have since seen many improvements in their lives. I have also suggested vaastu corrections to a great many people who have experienced positive benefits after the necessary changes were implemented. Seeing this success has cleared away any lingering doubts I might have had as to vaastu's effectiveness.

My personal experience, as well as my work with the Indus Valley Foundation, has made me something of an authority on vaastu in my own country. Now many of my Western friends have asked me to share that practical knowledge by writing a book on vaastu, so that others in the West could benefit from this ancient science. I take this request as an honor and a privilege, and I hope my honest attempt to fulfill this commitment will be taken in the same spirit by my readers.

THE INDIAN ART OF PLACEMENT

VAASTU IS A SANSKRIT WORD meaning "the science of structures." It is a traditional theory of architecture that guides the design and construction of buildings in harmony with the natural laws of the universe. As Einstein proved, everything in existence, sentient and nonsentient, is ultimately a field of energy. *Vastu* (with a single *a*) is the pure, subtle energy that underlies everything, while *vaastu* (with double *a*) is the manifestation or expression of that energy as matter. Every structure—whether it is a building or a fence, a statue or a piece of furniture, a piece of music or other art form—has its own subtle energy. Vaastu is the science of working with these fields of energy, guiding us to arrange structures so that their underlying energy fields are beneficially manipulated according to proportion and direction.

Although the term *vaastu* is often used today as a synonym for "building" or "architecture," vaastu relates not only to the design and construction of the building itself but also to such factors as interior decoration and the surrounding landscape. Vaastu describes desirable window and door locations, color schemes, symbols, artworks, and furniture arrangements. It also addresses the optimum type of soil, location of plants and water features, and construction of fences and compound walls. The science of vaastu is a meaningful dialogue between mind and nature, enabling us to better understand the energy fields of various objects around us as well as those of invisible cosmic bodies that affect our minds and bodies, influencing our lives directly and indirectly.

Vaastu considers a dwelling to be full of life force. It informs us how to make dwellings that have rhythm and beauty, that vibrate perfectly with nature. A structure built according to vaastu is considered a transformed entity, the life divine. At the same time, vaastu is a science based on vedic mathematics, one of the most advanced forms of knowledge in our universe. Thus the measuring system of vaastu is quite different from that of feng shui, which is not based on the same depth of calculations. In vaastu, each habitat has to be individualized, taking into consideration several significant factors, including orientation, direction, proportion, the activities performed within, and the personalities and vocations of the inhabitants.

Today many people are fortunate to enjoy abundant physical comforts as well as a long life, yet they feel inadequate and unhappy. They suffer from uneasiness in mind and body and do not seem to be in a balanced state of health. Often they are not helped by modern science, which is seriously lacking in its understanding of the connection and complex interaction between the mind and the body. Thus, it seems appropriate to look to the ancient Indian texts, the *Vedas*, for some of the answers. *Veda* literally means "science" or "knowledge." The *Vedas* are storehouses of knowledge concerning the intricate balance of the forces that affect human life and all of existence. This knowledge was revealed to humanity more than seven thousand years ago in the Himalayas. Despite their antiquity, the *Vedas* contain timeless knowledge of the expression of consciousness that can help us find answers to many of our modern concerns about health and life.

Vaastu is related to two other vedic sciences, jyotish (astrology) and ayurveda (lifestyle medicine). Jyotish—the science of stars and planets and their forces—teaches us about the subtle principles that affect and govern our physical and mental aspects. Ayurveda—the science of life—teaches us about the physical, physiological, and psychological makeup of these forces. It helps us to see that, in one sense, our own physical body is a perfect vaastu structure transformed into a living, vibrating entity. Vaastu—the science of physical structures—teaches us how to place or construct material structures, taking into account the planetary forces and their effects on our lives. When arranged and constructed according to these principles, our homes can be transformed into entities full of life energy. Jyotish, vaastu, and ayurveda work together to help us live more harmoniously and happily. Thus, this study of vaastu incorporates aspects of the other two sciences as well.

Part I of this book explains the philosophy and basic principles of vaastu in simple language, making it clear how the adoption of vaastu enables one to lead a healthy and contented life. Part II demonstrates how to apply vaastu principles to your home—its decoration, furnishings, interior design, and landscaping.

Parts III and IV are particularly for those who are designing and building new homes or planning extensive renovation of their existing home, as well as for professionals in the fields of interior design, architecture, and construction. Part III presents property and building site considerations and corrections. Part IV goes into detail regarding site preparation, construction principles, and design considerations such as the optimum location of particular types of rooms and the placement of doors and windows. Part V offers a sample consultation along with a comprehensive method of assessing buildings and land. It also contains a comparison of vaastu and feng shui.

This book provides many illustrations and anecdotes so that readers can readily learn how to apply this knowledge to their own situations. It also includes a grading system and tear-out score sheets to assess potential building sites and proposed house designs, thus facilitating the application of vaastu science to one's own dwelling and surroundings.

ENTERING THE WORLD OF VAASTU: FREQUENTLY ASKED QUESTIONS

THE FOLLOWING QUESTIONS AND ANSWERS PROVIDE an encapsulated overview to the subject of vaastu. In many cases the answer will point readers toward the specific chapter where the topic is discussed in greater detail.

Q: What is vaastu?
Vaastu is a traditional Indian theory of architecture that guides the design and construction of buildings in harmony with the natural laws of the universe. Vaastu science has its roots in the *Vedas,* dating back seven thousand years, and is very mathematical. It provides detailed information about how to select land, as well as how to design and construct buildings.

Q: How does vaastu help us?
Vaastu harmonizes our lives with nature, allowing us to unfold to our optimum potential.

Q: When do I need a vaastu consultation?
A vaastu consultation could be very helpful if you are purchasing or renting a house or designing a home. It is especially recommended if you are facing problems and hurdles in life, or if there is a lack of harmony at home or work.

Q: How long does it take to notice the benefits of good vaastu or vaastu rectifications?

If you are already facing problems, benefits could be noticed at any time—from immediately to a year or more later.

Q: What is the significance of the Vaastupurusha?

Vaastupurusha is the symbolic representation of all the physiological and psychological changes that take place within us as well as within a house. For more details on the meaning of Vaastupurusha and its significance, please see chapter 2, "The Story of Vaastupurusha."

Q: Why are the directions important in vaastu?

Different planets govern different directions and have specific influences on the inhabitants. By understanding the directions, one is able to able to balance the different forces harmoniously. (See chapter 4, "Directions, Dieties, and Planets.")

Q: According to vaastu, what do the various directions represent?

East governs prosperity, wisdom, and male issues.
Southeast governs health, fire, cooking, and food.
South governs wealth, crops, happiness, and the female head of the family.
Southwest governs character, behavior, longevity, and death.
West governs name, fame, prosperity, and the male head of the family.
Northwest governs change, income from business, enmity, and friendship.
North governs wealth, prosperity, and female issues.
Northeast governs health, wealth, spirituality, and all-around prosperity.

Q: What is the best direction for a house to face?

Each direction has an exalted position where the front entrance can be placed, and thus the house can face any direction. Chapter 22 describes good vaastu for doors, and figures 114–15 demonstrate exalted and debilitated positions.

Q: What are the things that are to be kept in mind while selecting a plot?

The major factors to be kept in mind while selecting a plot are geographical surroundings, level of the land, and roads around the plot. Scoresheet B in chapter 25 offers practical guidance in evaluating these factors.

Q: Do colors play a role in vaastu?

Yes. The colors in one's home or landscape should be coordinated with the colors of the respective planets and elements associated with different directions. Doing this will enhance the energy flow around the inhabitants. Chapter 7, "Interior Design," provides extensive details on color choices.

Q: How does vaastu affect me if I am living in a rental accommodation?
Vaastu principles affect you wherever you are living. Chapter 23 describes vaastu applications specific to apartments.

Q: How can vaastu be applied to commercial and industrial premises?
The science of vaastu is universal, and the basic principles given in this book are applicable to all types of buildings. Some specific points to keep in mind for commercial and industrial buildings are: inventory should ideally be placed in the Northwest sector to facilitate faster movement; equipment should be placed more to the Southwest and Southeast sides; chemicals should be stored underground in the Northeast. (See more on vaastu for commercial buildings in chapter 23.)

Q: What is the relationship between ayurveda and vaastu?
Ayurveda considers that our physiology and psychology are governed by three principles called *vaata*, *pitta,* and *kapha*, which in turn are represented by the five elements. *Vaata* is represented by space and air, *pitta* by fire and water, *kapha* by earth and water. Planetary forces in turn govern the elements. Nothing is apart from the other. Vaastu science is based on the interconnection and interplay of these factors in the one quantum soup that includes all existence.

Q: What is the role of religion in vaastu?
Religion plays no role in vaastu. Vaastu is based on universal principles of planetary forces and elements. Religion is based on an individual's beliefs.

Q: Is there a similarity between vaastu and solar home plans?
Yes. Both vaastu and solar home designs maximize the Sun's energy. Unlike solar home plans, vaastu works to maximize the energy of other planets as well.

Q: Are vaastu principles uniform throughout the world?
The principles of vaastu are based on energy flow and the distribution of elements. These factors are uniform throughout the world. However, in different geographical locations, the building could be designed to accommodate various climatic conditions while preserving good vaastu. For example, if you are living in the Northern hemisphere, far away from the equator, a Northeast front entrance door can be exchanged for a wide glass window to avoid the cold Northeasterly winds.

Q: As you go closer to the North or South Pole, the East and West directions merge. How does one identify the vaastu directions from there?
In keeping with ancient vaastu methodology, one must establish the direction of the East by using the help of a gnomon. A detailed explanation of how to use the gnomon is given in chapter 9, "Understanding Extension."

Q: How do changes in Earth's polarity affect vaastu?

There is scientific evidence that Earth's polarity changes once in twenty-five thousand years. However, there is no reference in any vaastu text linking its principles to Earth's magnetism. Vaastu is based purely on the interrelationship of planetary forces and their elemental principles. Hence, vaastu principles do not change with the change in Earth's polarity.

Q: What are the differences/similarities between vaastu and feng shui?

Feng shui is a Chinese art of placement. Vaastu is an Indian art of placement. Both have their roots in the knowledge of planetary energies and the basic elements governed by them. Feng shui takes into consideration wind, water, fire, and air as the basic elements, while vaastu takes into consideration space, air, fire, water, and earth. Vaastu is more mathematical than feng shui. The major difference between them lies in vaastu's detailed analysis of height/weight distribution, exalted/debilitated positions, and extensions and cuts. More details on their similarities and differences can be found in chapter 26, "Vaastu and Feng Shui."

PART ONE

THE PHILOSOPHY AND PRINCIPLES OF VAASTU

CHAPTER 1

THE HISTORY OF VAASTU

THE KNOWLEDGE OF VAASTU, like that of jyotish and ayurveda, was recorded in many ancient texts and has been an integral part of Indian culture for millennia. Maya—the great scientist, architect, and town planner of ancient India—presented its basic principles in the *Mayamatam,* the ancient treatise on vaastu rediscovered in 1934. Later this system was codified in the *Vaastu Veda* and *Sthapatya Veda.* While the *Vaastu Veda* deals with vaastu in relation to buildings, the *Sthapatya Veda* extends this consideration to music and poetry. In the old days the vaastu of buildings was practiced by carpenters known as *sthapathis*—sages who were also knowledgeable in astrology.

The excavations at Harappa and Mohenjodaro—which unearthed one of the most ancient human civilizations on the banks of the Indus River in Northwestern India—show that vaastu was extensively used. This level of architectural sophistication, complete with sewage systems, was unmatched in the world until the nineteenth century. In the centuries that followed, vaastu became more and more elaborate.

The great epics of India, the *Ramayana* and *Mahabharata,* include many instances of vaastu. For example, in the *Mahabharata,* Lord Krishna built his kingdom of Dwaraka according to vaastu tenets. Krishna wanted the kingdom to be sunk in the ocean after he finished his purpose on Earth (which was to destroy an evil warrior race called Yaadavas). Dwaraka's vaastu was apparently designed in such a way that it would last only for Krishna's lifetime. Soon after Krishna left his body, Dwaraka disappeared into the ocean. Recently the remnants of the city of Dwaraka have been discovered lying submerged in the Arabian Sea.

For the benefit of the readers who want to pursue further study, a list of well-known ancient vaastu books is given in Appendix A. There are several differences of opinion in these books, but all agree on the basic principles of vaastu that form the foundation of this workbook.

CHAPTER 2

THE STORY OF VAASTUPURUSHA

ONE OF THE ANCIENT TREATISES ON VAASTU, the *Brihat Samhita,* includes a myth about the origin of Vaastupurusha, the deity of vaastu. The god Shiva was once engaged in a battle with a demon. As the fierce struggle went on, Shiva began sweating profusely. Vaastupurusha was born out of Shiva's beads of sweat. His origin in strife made him very hungry and he started devouring everything in his path. The other gods went to Lord Brahma for protection, begging him to do something about this new creature that was destroying their world. Brahma gave Vaastupurusha a push and he fell to earth, landing face down. Immediately Brahma told the gods—who were forty-five in number—to sit on Vaastupurusha and not allow him to get up. After they did so, Vaastupurusha prayed for Brahma's mercy, entreating that he had been created hungry and that he was only following his nature. Brahma felt sorry for him and granted him the blessing of having his endless hunger fed by offerings from the inhabitants of the dwellings built upon him. In return, Vaastupurusha was to stay embedded in the earth and take care of the inhabitants' health and prosperity. But he could seek his own sustenance if the inhabitants didn't feed him properly. Those who did not abide by Brahma's rules would awaken the creature's hunger and suffer the consequences.

As with all myths, the true meaning of the symbol of Vaastupurusha is much deeper than the story. Understanding its importance will enable us to penetrate fur-

Fig. 1: Vaastupurusha

ther into the mysteries of life. The story of Vaastupurusha is our own story. A human being is both a material body *(vaastu)* and the subtle energy or spirit *(vastu* or *purusha)* within it. Similarly, Vaastupurusha can be seen as the living energy of a physical structure. In the same manner as our body and spirit are connected, the house (body) and Vaastupurusha (spirit) are connected. Vaastupurusha is nourished by the energy of the structure. If the physical layout of a dwelling fosters a flow of energy that supports the Vaastupurusha, then there is harmony within the house as well. Whenever there is a mismatch, there is disharmony. Whatever vibrations take place in the house eventually have an effect on the people who occupy the house.

The forty-five deities sitting on Vaastupurusha to restrain him represent our own angelic and demonic qualities that bind us to worldly life. When these qualities are properly understood and experienced, our life is harmonious and we enjoy health, peace, and prosperity. The house built following vaastu principles satisfies Vaastupurusha by allowing the flow of cosmic energy to be in balance and yield good things to the inhabitants.

By picturing Vaastupurusha lying facedown in his classic position, as shown in figure 1, and applying traditional Indian ayurvedic knowledge about different parts of the body, we can begin to see the proper roles for various sections of a house or plot. Vaastupurusha is understood to be lying facedown facing Northeast, the direction of wisdom and spirituality. That puts his right side to the East and South (representing *dakshina*) and his left side to the North (representing *uttara*) and West. In ayurveda the right side of the body represents masculine qualities, so when the life force is moving in the right side *(pingala)*, one is more active, critical, judgmental, and analytical. The left side of the body represents feminine qualities, so when the life force moves in that side *(ida)*, one's intuitive and compassionate nature dominates.

The *Brihat Samhita* describes a square or rectangular plot of land as ideal for the construction of a dwelling because Vaastupurusha's entire body fits within it, as in figure 1. If the square is incomplete—thus cutting off some part of Vaastupurusha—the inhabitants will suffer dire consequences. If Vaastupurusha has no right arm, they will lose wealth and the women will be miserable; if he has no left arm, there will be a loss of money and food. If his head is absent, the owner will suffer losses of virtue and prosperity. If his feet are missing, the male head of the family will become weak and the women will be troubled. On the other hand, if Vaastupurusha is endowed with all his limbs in fine shape, the inhabitants of the house will be famous and prosperous.

The ancient scriptures describe three different conditions regarding the position of Vaastupurusha's head:

1. *Nitya* (daily) *vaastu,* wherein Vaastupurusha alternates the position of his head between right and left approximately every three hours.
2. *Chara* (moving) *vaastu,* wherein Vaastupurusha changes his head position once every three months.
3. *Sthira* (nonmoving) *vaastu,* wherein Vaastupurusha's head is permanently established toward the Northeast direction.

Each of the three positions has great significance to our physical and spiritual health. The turning of Vaastupurusha's head in nitya vaastu signifies the alternation of the breath or *prana* (life force) between our right and left nostrils. Normally a healthy person breathes predominantly through one nostril or the other, alternating sides every three hours. The dominant side can be determined by holding a mirror in front of your nose while breathing once gently and then examining the moisture that has collected on the mirror. It will usually be uneven or one side will evaporate faster than the other. The side that evaporates more slowly reveals the dominant nostril. Knowledge of this movement of prana is called *Swarashastra* (science of breath and consciousness). The movement of the life force in a person is very significant in relation to one's feelings and emotions as well as to one's health, spirituality, and prosperity. In nitya vaastu the energy movement in the house is in tune with the energy movement of the inhabitants. This synergy of energy is key to health and contentment.

Chara vaastu signifies the seasonal changes that take place in our constitution. According to ayurveda, each person's constitution is composed of varying amounts of three principles known as the *dhaatus (vaata, pitta,* and *kapha)*. These three principles govern all of the physiological and psychological aspects of our existence (described in more detail in the next chapter, "Basis of Balanced Life"). The movement of Vaastupurusha's head every three months symbolizes the effect of the seasons on the *dhaatus*. From March to June, Vaastupurusha's gaze is to the North and *kapha* is predominant, moving toward *pitta*. From June to September, Vaastupurusha's gaze is to the East and *pitta* is predominant, moving toward *vaata*. From September to December, Vaastupurusha's gaze is to the South, and from December to March it is to the West, during which *vaata* is becoming predominant and then moving toward *kapha*. Thus seasonal changes can create imbalance in the *dhaatus* of the inhabitants. This can be counteracted by balancing the energy flow of the house between these three principles according to vaastu.

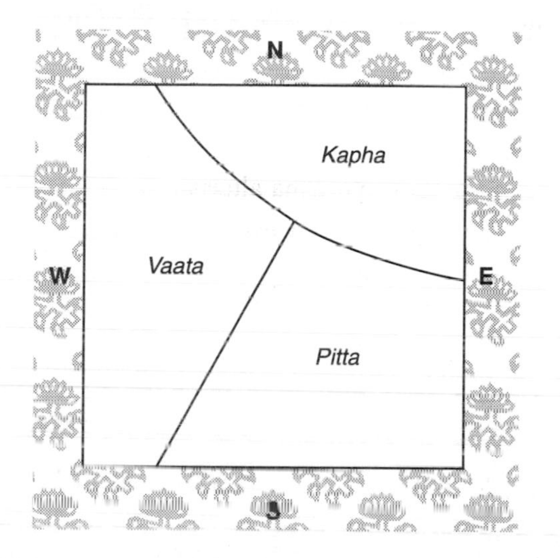

Fig. 2: ***Vaata, pitta,*** **and** ***kapha*** **zones**

In sthira vaastu Vaastupurusha's head is fixed toward the Northeast, the direction governed by the two planets of wisdom and knowledge—Jupiter and Ketu (described in more detail in chapter 4, "Directions, Deities, and Planets"). It thus signifies one's commitment to wisdom and knowledge leading to enlightenment, fostered by the energy in a good vaastu home.

CHAPTER 3

BASIS OF BALANCED LIFE: THE VEDIC SCIENCES OF AYURVEDA, JYOTISH, AND VAASTU

THE FOUNDATION OF LIFE is self-knowledge—understanding our existence in totality. This understanding of the deeper structure of existence is essential for a harmonious life, yet modern scientific knowledge gives us only a limited view of our total reality. The vedic seers, on the other hand, knew that all material forms are nothing but the expressions of cosmic consciousness and the manifestation of the divine. The *Vedas* declare that the answer to the secret of creation was given to the sages by Lord Shiva in codified form:

> *Nrittavasane natarajarajah nanadadhakkam nava panchavaram*
> *Udhartukamah sanakadisiddan etadvimarshe sivasutrajalam.*
>
> *Lord Shiva at the end of his divine cosmic dance,*
> *out of pure compassion towards the great seers like Sanaka*
> *gave the secret of creation by sounding the drum nine and five times.*

With their extraordinary brilliance the sages understood that the sounding of the drum nine times represented the nine planetary forces that control, operate, and guide everything. They also understood that the sounding of the drum five times represented the five elements that form the building blocks for all material existence—ether, air, fire, water, and earth. They saw the harmonious connection and complex interplay between energy and matter. This fundamental knowledge later became the basis for the sciences of ayurveda, jyotish, and vaastu, which individually and synergistically guide us to participate in the harmonious operation of the universe.

Jyotish describes the logistics of the planetary forces and how they operate. Ayurveda tells us in what proportion and through which elements those forces should function for optimum health. Vaastu guides us in harmonizing these energies through structures and arrangements. When these forces are allowed to express themselves properly, a perfect natural order gets established. Thus, the three sciences are the knowledge base for holistic understanding of our existence and wellness.

If we think of our physical body (described by ayurveda) as being like a television, its antenna would be the operation of subtle energy (vaastu) and the broadcasting frequency would be the forces described by astrology (jyotish). For one to receive a perfect picture on the television (equal to peace and prosperity in life), all three components—the television, the antenna, and the broadcasting frequency—must be in proper order. A defect in any of the three may give a poor quality picture, which represents an unbalanced life. Thus, even if one has a good destiny as demonstrated by his astrological chart (comparable to good quality broadcasting), he still needs to observe the tenets of ayurveda to maintain his physical health (keep the television in good repair) and live in a good vaastu home (have a good antenna) to reap the full benefits.

One of my clients was a person whose experiences demonstrate this relationship. He had very good planetary positions in his horoscope. But he had been an alcoholic for twenty years, which had left him financially devastated. When I looked at the vaastu of his house I noticed it had many defects. It had a hill to the North and a well to the Northern Northwest—defects that negatively impact the inhabitants in terms of financial losses and addictions. In addition, the Southeast was lower than the Northwest and Northeast. Vaastu maintains that this brings bad character and bad luck to the second son. My client was the second son of his parents, so I advised him to move out of the house and sell the property. He followed my advice, selling the house and moving to a smaller but perfect vaastu house where none of the defects of his previous house existed. After a few slips during the first year, he slowly and steadily progressed. By the end of the second year he had totally given up alcohol. The effect of the vaastu alone was sufficient to bring about this significant change. During the third year he and his family moved to another correct vaastu house in a different city where he started his own business. The business is prospering, his family is doing well, and he is well liked and respected in society.

Our destiny operates through the principles expressed as the five basic elements—ether, air, fire, water, and earth. From the smallest particle of matter to the grossest body such as a star or a planet, all are governed by these five underlying principles. According to the *Vedas* there is nothing beyond these five principles in the physical world. Under varying conditions these principles attract, repel, bind, and blend with one another in unending ways, always following perfect logistics. Understanding their logistics is the key to leading a harmonious, healthy life.

The *Vedas* explain that ether (*akasha*) is the pure space that first manifests from consciousness. But this pure space is not nothingness; it is full of particles. As subatomic physics explains, the very first manifestation of matter is both a wave and a particle, depending on the observer's point of view, changing from energy to matter and matter to energy in less than a billionth of a second. Our mind and thoughts are comparable to ether. When ether becomes more condensed, atoms and molecules are produced. This principle is called air *(vaayu).* Air should not be confused with hydrogen, nitrogen, oxygen, or many other gases. They are all part of the air principle, which is movement. When the movement becomes very strong, heat is generated. This principle of heat is called fire *(agni).* Fire is the principle of metabolism in all sentient beings and heat in the nonsentient. From fire, the water principle *(jala)* is born. One may wonder how fluidity can come from heat. The ordinary knowledge of physics tells us that when hydrogen (air principle) burns, water is produced. Also, intense heat liquefies many metals. This liquid or fluid state of matter is the water principle. From it, the earth principle *(prithvi)* evolves. Earth represents the solid state of matter, something that is heavy and grounded. Thus, our universe is composed of the five basic elements.

Our body, mind, and spirit are also made up of these five elements at both the gross and subtle (astral) levels. Our five sense objects—ear, skin, eyes, tongue, and nose—and their underlying qualities *(tanmatras)*—sound, touch, vision, taste, and smell—are governed by the subtle principles of the five elements. Sound is governed by the space principle and touch by the air principle. The fire principle governs vision, the water principle governs taste, and the earth principle governs smell.

Senses	Tanmatras	Elements
Ears	Sound	Space
Skin	Touch	Air
Eyes	Vision	Fire
Tongue	Taste	Water
Nose	Smell	Earth

According to ayurveda all of the biological activities of our body and mind are governed by the three principles of *vaata, pitta,* and *kapha. Vaata* governs all movements such as breathing and the circulation of all nutrients and waste products in the body. *Vaata* is mainly composed of the elements ether and air. *Pitta*—which governs all metabolic activities, the conversion of nutrients into various tissues in the body, and mental comprehension—is mainly composed of the fire and water elements. *Kapha*—which acts as a binding principle and provides tissue sustenance in the body—is the product of the earth and water elements.

The celestial bodies are also composed of the five elements. The planetary forces described by astrology are thus governed by the subtle nature of the elements. Based on their elemental composition, different planets and stars emanate different grades of energies. These energies have different influences on us, depending on the planets' proximity to each other, their size, the direction in which they are moving, and the speed at which they are rotating. The Sanskrit word for astrology, *jyotish,* means "guiding light to the secrets of creation." Its literal translation *(jyotir vishaya)* is "the information of the light," in which light signifies the manifestation of consciousness. The vedic seers postulated that life is not just something that manifests in different bodies. In their deep meditation and through their intuitive knowledge, they traced the intricate and complex astral connections between our lives and various heavenly bodies such as planets and stars.

The vedic philosophy says that each individual's actions (both good and bad) create a certain pattern called *karma.* These karmas are carried in the hidden energy at the base of one's spine, called *kundalini.* An individual takes birth based on the accumulated karma of the past and this determines the time, date, and place of birth. The various planets and stars that are in a particular combination at the time of birth (documented by one's natal chart) determine one's course of life. This blueprint of an individual constitutes jyotish, vedic astrology.

As much as these planets and stars affect our lives directly, they also impact us indirectly through structures and symbols. Houses and other buildings, temples, townships, and even idols and statues all are influenced by these forces. When properly created and arranged, a structure will harmonize all the energies of the planets to produce a beneficial vibration that will foster the best possible result within the limits of one's karma. Guiding this is the role of the science of vaastu.

Just as solar home designs take into consideration the movement of the sun, the amount of sunshine, and the direction providing the maximum number of hours of sunlight, the sun is a major consideration in vaastu homes as well. However, vaastu also takes into consideration the subtle influence of the other planetary forces in our solar system.

Vaastu is profound and deep-rooted. It provides for a clear expression of the five elements in a structure, enabling it to become a living, vibrating entity. The arrangement of different elements in different proportions and shapes is what determines how the energies flow through a structure. Understanding how to make a house harmonious with other living, vibrating structures (the inhabitants) is the science of vaastu, which has proven itself to be very accurate and reproducible. When all the elements are properly arranged, a structure becomes a vaastu house.

Thus the three vedic sciences—jyotish, vaastu, and ayurveda—are all significant in understanding how we function as part of the universe. This understanding of our holistic makeup is the key to living in a balanced state of well-being, enjoying a happy, healthy, and prosperous life.

CHAPTER 4

DIRECTIONS, DEITIES, AND PLANETS

THE PRINCIPLES OF VAASTU are derived from the relationships between the spatial directions and the deities and planets that govern them. The influence of these relationships on a piece of property or a structure can best be understood when illustrated as in figure 3, showing the different directional sectors. The example given is for a square plot. Other shapes must be carefully dealt with and the sections that follow give detailed instructions on how to handle them. However, similar rules apply to all shapes, and in all cases the intersection of North-South and East-West must be at the center of the plot.

Each direction, such as North or East, is divided into nine divisions. The two outer divisions become part of the particular sector, such as Northeast or Southeast, and the middle five divisions become that particular direction. For example, in the North, the right two divisions become Northern Northeast and the left two divisions become Northern Northwest. Among the middle five divisions the right two-and-a-half divisions belong to the Northeastern sector and are called Northeastern North, while the two-and-a-half divisions to the left of the middle belong to the Northwestern North.

The chart also shows the deities and planets associated with each sector. A brief description of their properties and how they affect a structure is given below, as this provides the firm logical ground for the practical application of vaastu given in the rest of the book.

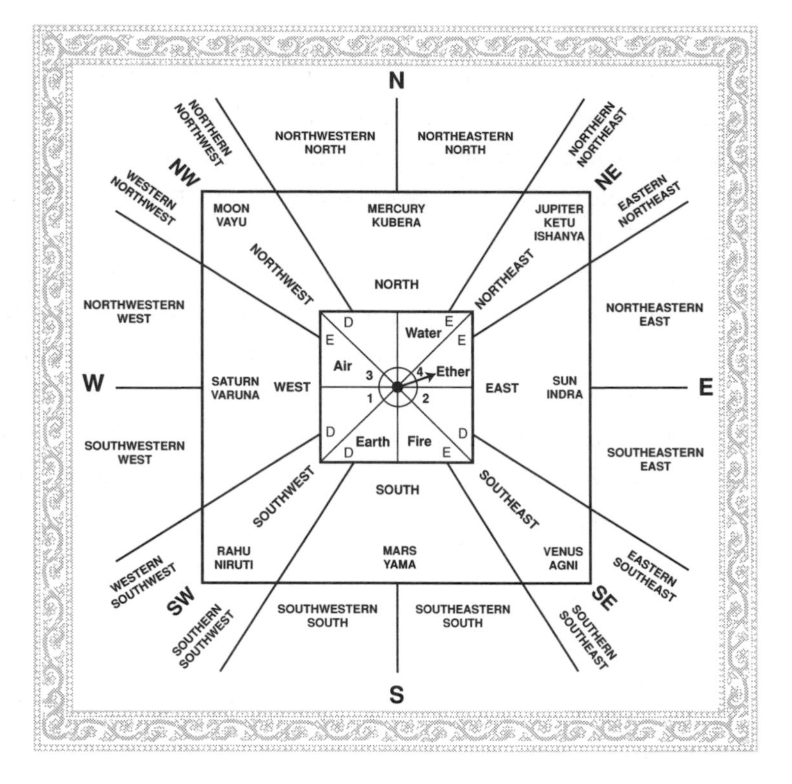

Fig. 3: Reading Directions

DIRECTION: EAST

Deity: Indra

Planet: Sun

The deity of the East is Indra, who bestows royal and religious qualities and stimulates creative and positive thinking. The Sun (Aditya) is the governing planet. The Sun represents the fire element and is the giver of health and the destroyer of all obstacles. On the physical level the Sun rules the heart, circulation, digestion, the nervous system, the immune system, eyesight, and bones. It governs a person's potential—their intelligence, perceptions, character, and endurance. The Sun is considered as the self *(atma)* and represents ego, power, prestige, fame, authority, and control. Positive signs of the Sun's influence are self-confidence, a strong will, courage, leadership, and straightforwardness.

If negated, the Sun could cause low self-esteem and the lack of motivation, courage, stamina, intelligence, and perception. If, on the other hand, it is too strong, it can make one highly domineering, egotistic, and foolish, lacking a sense of discrimination.

How these qualities govern an individual is determined astrologically. However, one has the capacity to modify or nullify them at the individual level through vaastu. For example, if the Sun's force is weak in one's chart, one can counteract it by living in a house or working in a place that conforms to a good vaastu on the East side. On the other hand, a vaastu defect on the East side may cause many difficulties to the inhabitants, regardless of their chart. They may suffer from low energy or become chronically ill, and the male inhabitants may even die prematurely. Financial difficulties and failures in all spheres of life are common occurrences in homes with Eastern vaastu defects.

One house I was called to for vaastu consultation had every possible defect on the Eastern side. The kitchen and bathrooms were on the Northeast side. The Northeast was closed, a condition that chokes the prosperity and health of the inhabitants. The main entrance was in the Southwest, a condition that brings financial losses and accidents. During the first week after the family moved into the house, the owner slipped in the house and broke his leg. The West was lower than the East, a factor that discouraged male family members from living there. Only two sisters lived in the home, both experiencing difficulties in their careers, severe financial difficulties, and low energy.

There was no possibility of correcting these defects, short of demolition and reconstruction. The family decided to sell the property and moved into another house with correct vaastu. Within six months, things started to improve and the family is prospering. Their health is improving and they are experiencing contentment in life.

DIRECTION: SOUTHEAST

Deity: Agni

Planet: Venus

The deity of the Southeast is Agni (fire), who governs knowledge, judgment, and discrimination. The governing planet for the Southeast is Venus. She represents the water element that regulates the metabolic fire that transforms our food to *tejas* (energy) and *ojas* (creative force). Thus, Venus ultimately controls the immunity of the body and the clarity of the mind. Physically, Venus directly influences the energy level of the person. The main organs governed by Venus are those of the genitourinary systems. She governs beauty, charm, and grace, as well as relationships with the opposite sex, romantic life, and the expression of feelings. The beneficial influence of Venus brings good taste and a refined personality. Venus predominantly affects the second child of a family.

A house built with a correct vaastu of the Southeast delivers good health to the inhabitants, while a defective Southeast may cause accidental fires, robberies, cancer, kidney problems, disorders of the reproductive organs, low energy levels, digestive disorders, and diseases related to disorders in the immune system. One's relationship with loved ones is disturbed because Venus governs one's expressive ability. Vaastu defects in the Southeast cause constant disagreements among family members, who become too judgmental. For example, a door in the Eastern Southeast causes constant bickering and rivalry between the members of the family.

Once, I was driving with a friend of mine in a nice neighborhood. I saw a beautiful house that had a gate and front door in Eastern Southeast. I mentioned to my friend, who happened to know the family, that this vaastu defect would cause the family members to have disagreements. He told me that, in fact, the couple was thinking of getting a divorce. Later I heard that the family corrected the defect and are now living happily. Another house I recently visited has a small Southeast defect of the kind that creates fire hazards according to vaastu. When I mentioned this to the owner, he told me that the house had been totally burned and then rebuilt a few years before he bought it. Vaastu effects are not always immediate, especially in the case of minor defects. In this particular case, the fire accident took place only fifty years after the defect was constructed.

DIRECTION: SOUTH

Deity: Yama

Planet: Mars

The governing deity for the South side is Yama, the upholder of *dharma* (virtue). He is introspective, impartial, and withdrawn. He is also known as the god of death who is the final judge of all our deeds in life. The Southern direction is governed by the planet Mars, a planet of great energy that represents the fire element. Mars controls motivation and one's capacity to project emotions and passions. The energy to drive toward success and the ability to carry things out to completion are influenced by Mars. Physically, Mars governs the immune system, appetite, absorption of food, the liver, and small intestines.

A vaastu free of defects on the South side of a home brings peace and prosperity to the inhabitants, while defective vaastu of the South side can lead to accidents and violent deaths, engaging in wars and gang activities, bleeding disorders, slow healing of wounds, anemia, and impotence.

I know of several families whose homes had vaastu defects of the South and who have suffered heavily, with experiences similar to the ones I have narrated in my own story. A close member of my family whose house had a well in the South died in a violent accident a few years ago. Before that he had suffered two major auto accidents along with his wife and children. After the death of the husband, the wife and children moved into a good vaastu house with a Northeast entrance, Southeast kitchen, and Southwest bedroom. The family has since prospered, experiencing no financial problems. Life is moving smoothly and the children are doing well in school.

DIRECTION: SOUTHWEST

Deity: Niruti

Planet: Rahu (North Lunar Node)

The governing deity of the Southwest is Niruti. Depression, sleep, sadness, and grieving are his qualities. Rahu, the governing planet of the Southwest direction, represents the air element and controls one's mental and psychic faculties. As Rahu is considered to be a malefic planet, great care must be exercised to make sure that the Southwest does not have any vaastu defects. The vaastu effects of the Southwest mainly impact the heads of the family.

On the positive side, a well-balanced vaastu in the Southwest brings good mental stability and heightens one's astral sensitivity and awareness, popularity, prestige, and fame. On the other hand, a Southwest defect can cause cloudy perceptions, hallucinations, unexplainable unhappiness, irritability, anxiety, and fear, leading to suicidal tendencies, melancholic personalities, drug addictions, violent accidents, and deaths.

When I heard that a very close childhood friend of mine had died prematurely, I suspected a Southwest defect. Later, when I visited the house, I noticed there was an open well in the Southwest, a serious vaastu defect. The kitchen was in the Northeast, which has the effect of causing the premature death of male family members. Following my advice, my friend's wife sold her house and moved into a new house designed according to vaastu tenets by my wife and me. The family is doing well in the new house; the daughter of the family married and is living happily.

DIRECTION: WEST

Deity: Varuna

Planet: Saturn

The deity of the West is Varuna, who is compassionate and giving. Saturn, a very strong planet, is the governing planet for the West side. Both his negative and positive effects are extreme. Delaying and withholding are his nature. He brings detachment, desire for solitude, and a yearning for realization of the truth. Saturn rules over death, disease, poverty, separation, ugliness, and dirt. As Saturn represents the air element, he governs *vaata*-related diseases such as arthritis. Saturn also controls the nervous system and the psyche. On the positive side Saturn brings order, stability, a good reputation, peace, prosperity, magnanimity, detachment, and independence. Selfishness, egotism, doubts, fantasies, fear, phobia, and perversity are also related to Saturn.

From the vaastu perspective, construction on the West side should be heavier—

that is, it should have less open space—than on the East and North sides. Garbage and dirt should be placed at the West side. The West represents the male, so vaastu defects in the West particularly affect the male members of the family, bringing unpleasant to violent responses such as illness, injury, and—in extreme cases—death to the male head of the family.

DIRECTION: NORTHWEST

Deity: Vaayu

Planet: Moon

Both the deity and the planet of the Northwest—Vaayu (air) and the Moon—govern the mind, emotions, and moods. The Moon influences aspects of interpersonal relationships such as intimacy, friendship, and attachment. Contentment in life and the ability to withstand strain and stress are also governed by the Moon. These positive qualities are enhanced when the Moon is strong in one's natal chart and vaastu of the Northwest is not defective. On the negative side, a defective vaastu causes emotional instability, moodiness, depression, negativity, lethargy, and dullness.

Physically the Moon governs bodily fluids and is thus related to anemia, edema, dehydration, skin dryness, and constipation. She also governs the lungs and kidneys. Asthma, bronchitis, accumulation of phlegm, and obesity are common to the inhabitants when the Northwest of a dwelling is defective.

DIRECTION: NORTH

Deity: Kubera

Planet: Mercury

The deity Kubera, the god of wealth, governs the North. The planet of the North, Mercury, governs commerce and investment, education, intellectual powers such as comprehension and calculation, and communication skills such as writing, ease of expression, and tact. A good vaastu of the North brings the positive expressions of these qualities and bountiful prosperity. On the negative side, a defective Northern vaastu results in the lack of intellectual skills, fickleness, irrationality, financial loss, poverty, addictions, and lack of self-control.

Mercury represents the water element and in the body he governs the heart, nervous system, digestive system, and skin. If there is a defect in the North, one could suffer from nervous disorders such as anxiety, insomnia, tremors, palpitations, itchy dry skin, and irritable bowel syndrome, or from allergies or heart- and lung-related ailments.

I have consistently seen many families who have defects in the North having problems. One house whose occupants I consulted with has a Northern Northwest door, a defect that causes mental instability and loss of character. After moving to that house the man became very unpredictable and moody. He started having extramarital affairs and his life became a total mess. Recently the family moved out of the house and the affairs came to an end.

A few months ago an old gentleman was building a small underground water tank at the Northern Northwest side of his home. I advised him not to build the tank and explained that a pit or a well in Northwest brings sudden financial losses and bad health. However, he built the tank anyway. Within a few weeks he suffered a heavy financial loss due to an extended hospitalization. Since then, he has corrected the defect. Now his business has improved and life is going smoothly.

In another incident, a family moved into a huge newly built bungalow. The property had a road on the North side. The house was built close to the road, leaving less space in the North and more space in the South, a vaastu defect. Within a few months of moving into the house, the head of the family suffered heavy financial losses and a nervous breakdown. After suffering for three years, he moved to a good vaastu house with a more spacious and open North and all his problems have been resolved.

DIRECTION: NORTHEAST

Deity: Ishanya

Planets: Jupiter and Ketu

The deity governing Northeast is Ishanya, the giver of spirituality and fortune. Two planets govern the Northeast—Jupiter and Ketu (South Lunar Node or Dragon's Tail). Jupiter is the giver of joy and positive spirit; he is the optimist who sees good in everything. Known in Sanskrit as *Guru* (a spiritual master who bestows divine grace), Jupiter guides one to turn all adversities into positive learning experiences. Jupiter represents the element ether and fosters one's physical health by giving strength, vitality, and immunity. He also controls fortune, wealth, and success.

Ketu—who represents the fire element—governs all wisdom and helps one to reach the highest pinnacles of spirituality. He is known to be the deliverer of *moksha* (the final realization of truth).

Defects in the Northeast severely affect one's progeny and prosperity. The negative aspect of Ketu causes infertility and makes inhabitants negative, critical, doubting, foolish, and isolated. Family members may suffer from financial difficulties, anxiety, depression, lack of self-esteem, low energy level, and self-pity, or from poor liver and pancreatic functioning.

CHAPTER 5

BASIC PRINCIPLES OF VAASTU

THE APPLICATION OF VAASTU is based on three fundamental principles: 1) height and weight (referring to the amount of open space); 2) slopes and elevations; and 3) exalted and debilitated positions. The thorough understanding of these principles—which are similar to formulas in mathematics—is essential to understanding vaastu.

All classical texts and contemporary vaastu practitioners agree on the first two principles, but there is some disagreement over the exalted and debilitated positions, even among the classical texts. For example, the *Brihat Samhita* says that the exalted positions are on the Western Southwest and Northern Northwest sides, but this is the exact opposite view of our modern-day vaastu understanding. The *Brihat Samhita* perspective is based on the presiding deities in each of the nine squares in each direction, while the modern view is based on the principle of height and weight and the principle of slopes, as well as on the energy flow between planets (see chapter 6, "The Relationship of Vaastu to Yantra, Mantra, and Tantra"). My vaastu teacher firmly believes in this concept, which conforms to other vaastu principles. My personal experience of applying it has also proved consistently successful. On the other hand, if one follows the *Brihat Samhita* analysis of exalted positions, many inconsistencies arise, and it is not possible to follow the logistics of planetary influences with the height and weight principle.

Therefore, in this book we will adhere to the modern interpretations of the cardinal principles of vaastu that can be universally applied to town planning, large and small plots, houses, interiors, and landscaping.

THE PRINCIPLE OF HEIGHT AND WEIGHT

Figure 4 illustrates the ideal emphasis of height and weight according to vaastu.

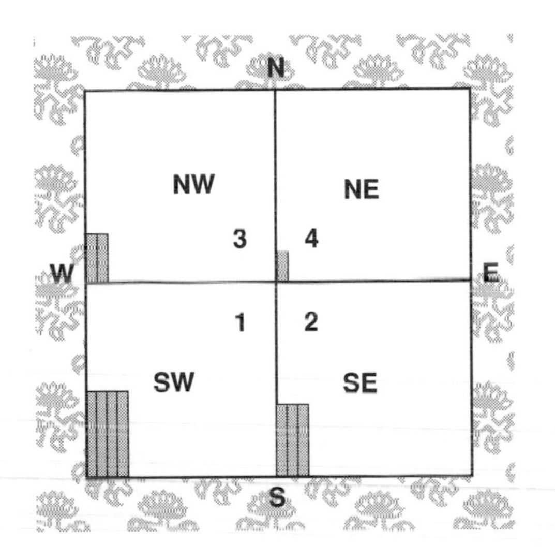

Fig. 4: Applying the height and weight principle

1. South and West should be heavy (with less open space) and at a higher elevation.
2. North and East should be lighter (with more open space) and at a lower elevation.
3. North should be lower than South.
4. North should be lighter (with more open space) than South.
5. East should be lower than West.
6. East should be lighter (with more open space) than West.
7. In general it is considered good vaastu if an area is sloping toward Northeast from Southwest.
8. Southwest should be highest in height and heaviest in weight (with least open space).
9. Southeast should be second highest in height and weight.
10. Northwest should be third highest in height and weight.
11. Northeast should be lowest in height and weight.

THE PRINCIPLE OF SLOPES AND ELEVATIONS

Slopes or lower elevations bring in more energy. As more positive energy comes to a house from the East and the North, those directions should be lower and have more slope than the West and the South. The South and the West have more negative energy, so a higher elevation and less slope on those sides will reduce the negative energy coming to the house.

The roof of a building can be flat or, if it has a slope, it should follow the vaastu principles expressed in figures 7–12. In any event, the South should not slope more than the North, and the West should not slope more than the East.

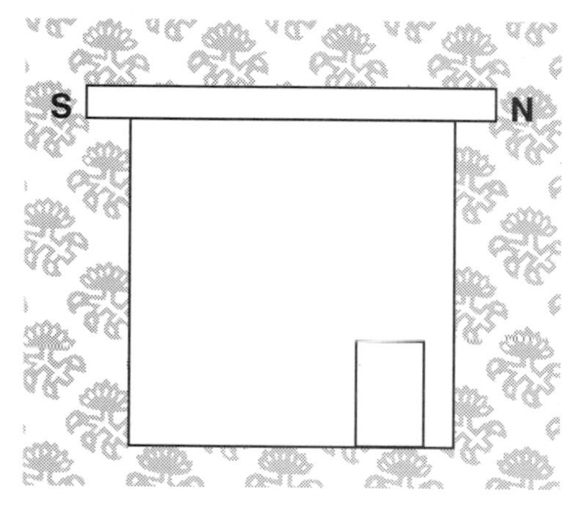

Fig. 5: The roof level is flat from South to North and there is no slope—it is acceptable.

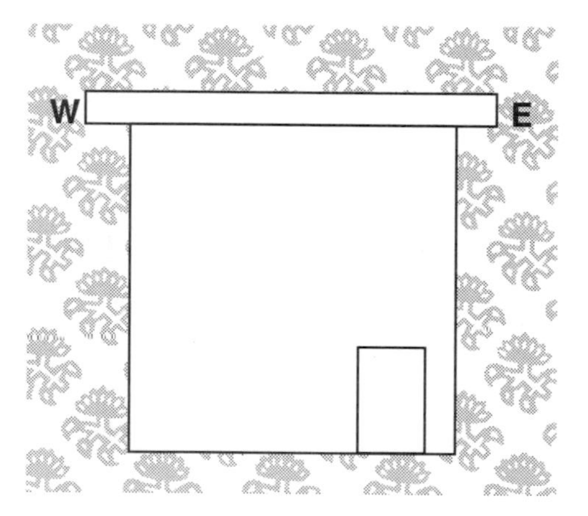

Fig. 6: The roof level is flat from West to East and there is no slope—it is acceptable.

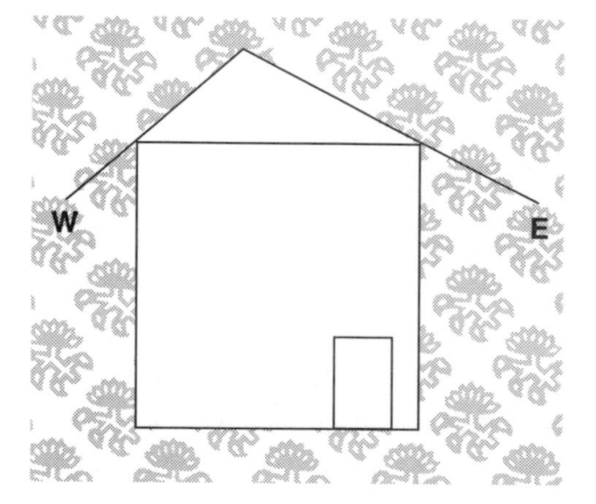

Fig. 7: Larger slope on the East than on the West—this is a good vaastu feature.

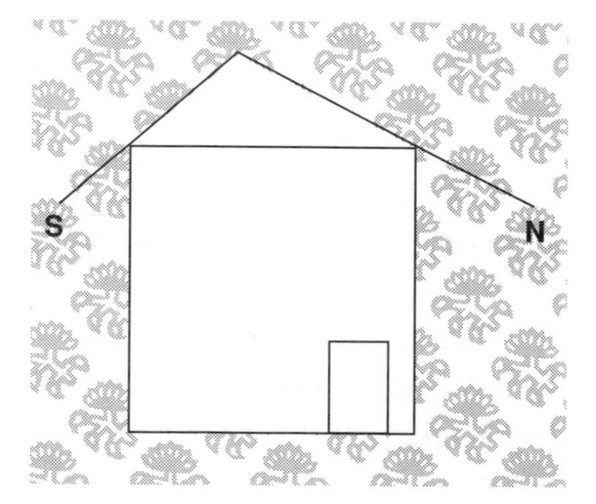

Fig. 8: Larger slope on the North than on the South—this is a good feature.

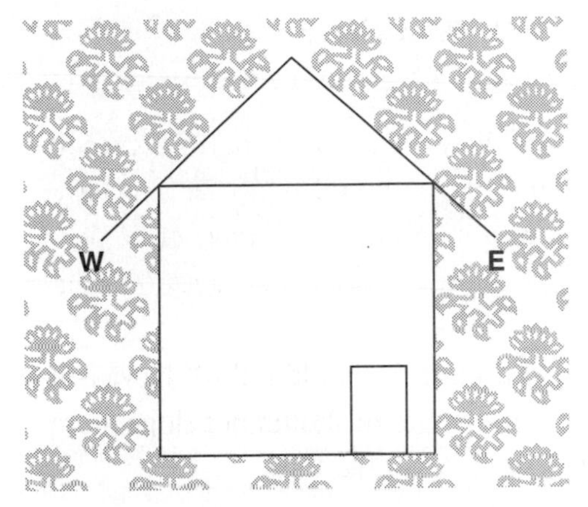

Fig. 9: West and East are equally sloped—it is balanced and acceptable.

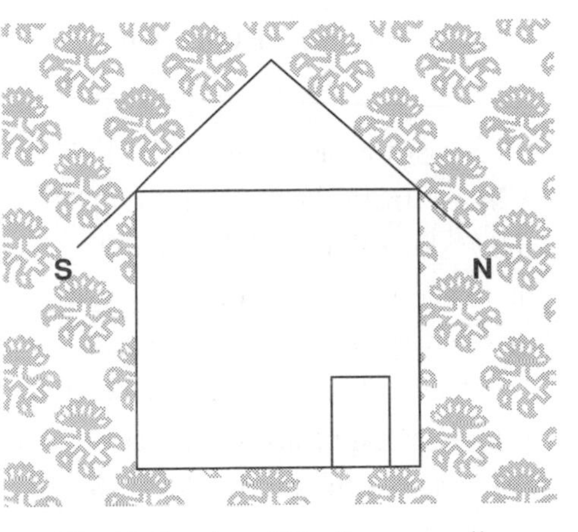

Fig. 10: South and North are equally sloped—it is balanced and acceptable.

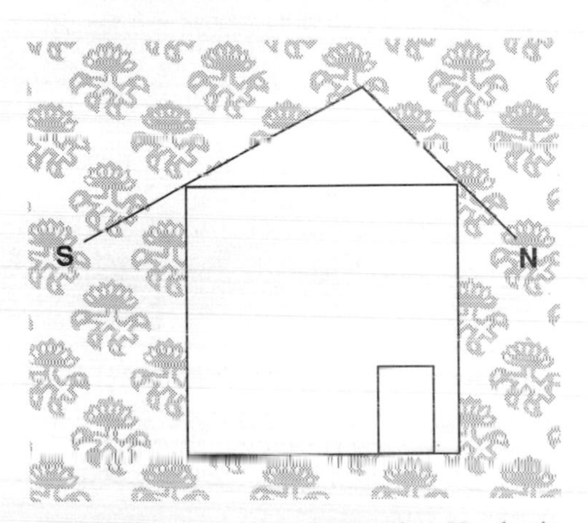

Fig. 11: South is more sloping than North—it is not acceptable.

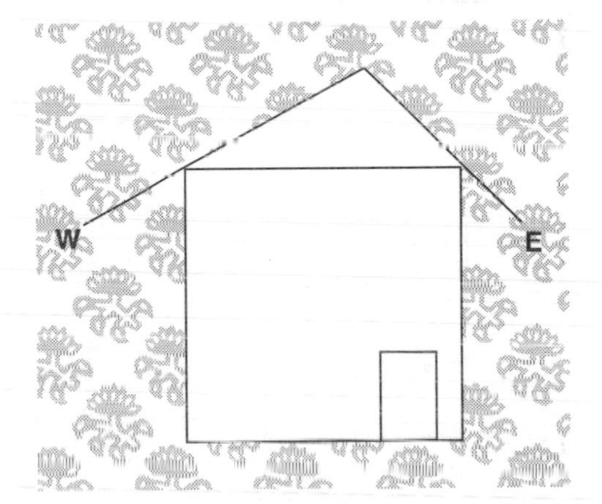

Fig. 12: West is more sloping than East—it is not acceptable.

THE PRINCIPLE OF EXALTED AND DEBILITATED POSITIONS

The third important vaastu principle is that of the exalted *(ucha)* and debilitated *(neecha)* positions, depicted in figures 13 and 14. The determination of exalted and debilitated positions is especially significant in the positioning of doors, windows, and gates. The application of the nodern view of exalted and debilitated positions works as follows: on the East side, the height and elevation increase from the Northeast to the Southeast; the exalted position is up to the midpoint starting from the North end. Similarly, on the South side, the height and elevation increase toward the West. From the East end, the exalted position is up to the midpoint on the South side. If you follow the same logic on the West side, the height and elevation increase from the North end to the South end, and naturally the exalted position should be from the North end to the midpoint toward the South. On the North side the height and elevation increase from the East to the West end and it is logical that the point starting from the East end running toward the West up to the midpoint becomes exalted.

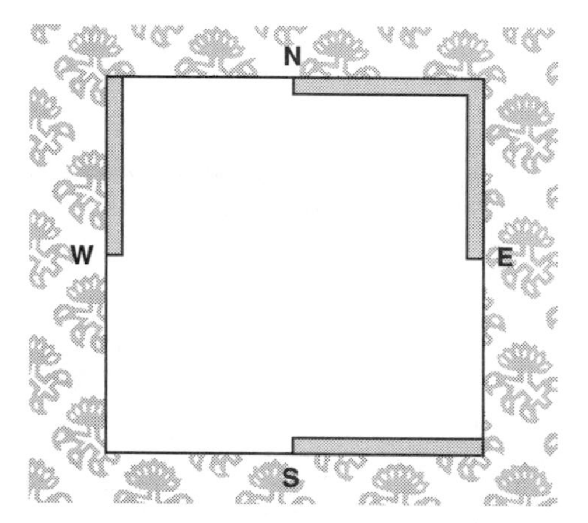

Fig. 13: Exalted *(ucha)* positions

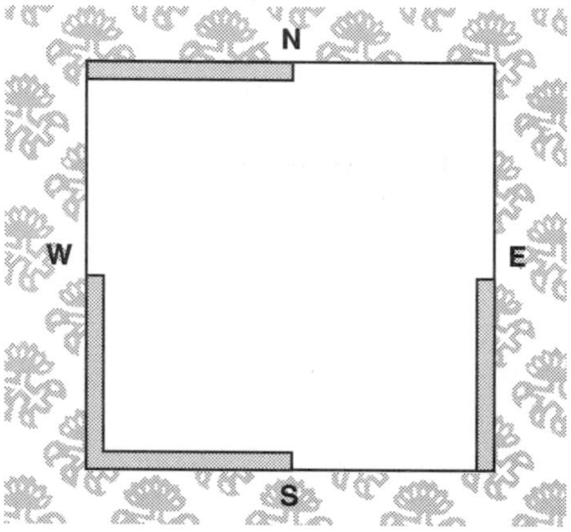

N
W
E
S

Fig. 14: Debilitated *(neecha)* positions

To correctly assess the exalted and debilitated positions, the area being considered is divided precisely according to the tenets of vaastu. The area may be a square or rectangle and may be rotated up to 45 degrees.

Figure 15 shows a square divided into four equal quadrants. These quadrants come into play in most vaastu considerations, but generally plots will not be perfectly square or perfectly oriented along the meridians. When dividing irregular plots into quadrants, the division should always be from the center point of the plot. If the plot is rotated, the sizes of the quadrants will be unequal, such as these in figure 16, rotated 25 degrees. In another example where the plot is diagonally rotated 45 degrees (fig. 17), all of the sectors are triangular.

The basis for the assessment of exalted and debilitated positions is a square set perfectly to North, as in figure 18. The midpoints of all four sides are joined by lines that intersect at the midpoint. This divides the square into four quadrants, namely Northeast, Southeast, Southwest, and Northwest. Then each quadrant is divided into two halves by joining the four corners.

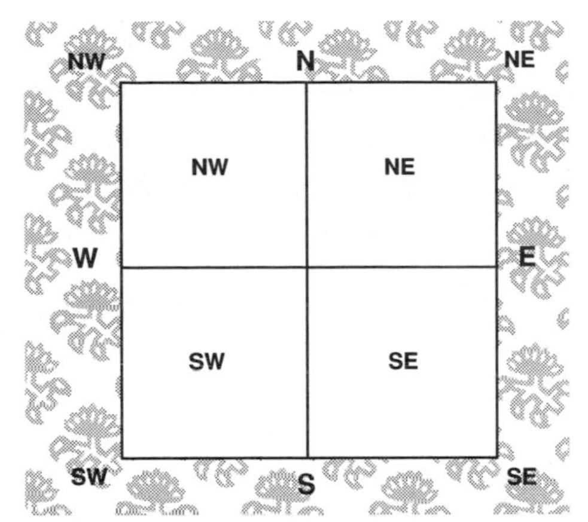

Fig. 15: Square divided into four equal quadrants

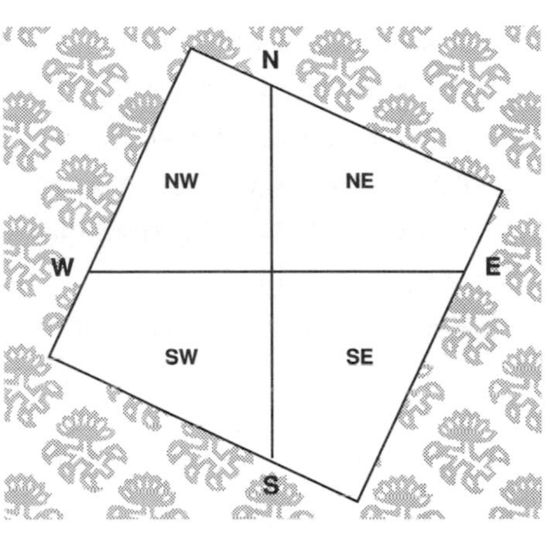

Fig. 16: Clockwise rotation of the plot by 25 degrees

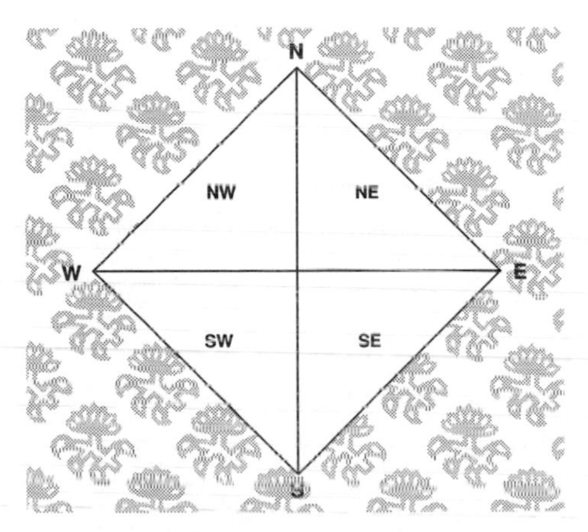

Fig. 17: Plot rotated by 45 degrees

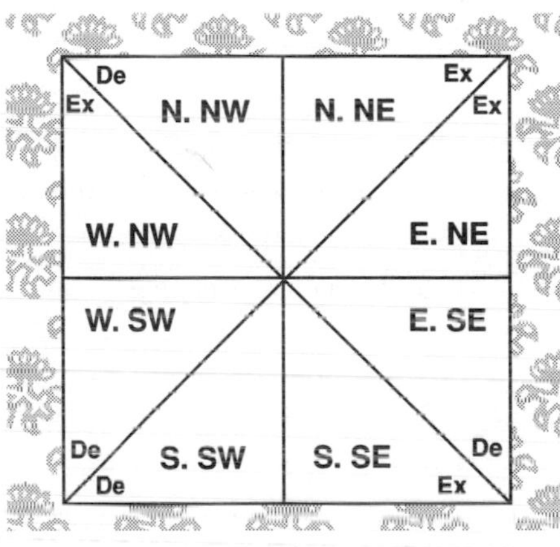

Fig. 18: Square set to North (De – Debilitated; Ex – Exalted)

The exalted and debilitated positions are as follows:

In the Northeast sector both Northern Northeast and Eastern Northeast are exalted.

In the Southeast sector, Eastern Southeast is debilitated and Southern Southeast is exalted.

In the Southwest sector, both Southern Southwest and Western Southwest are debilitated.

In the Northwest sector, Western Northwest is exalted and Northern Northwest is debilitated.

If the plot is a rectangle set in the East–West direction, as shown in figure 19, different results are obtained.

Northeast in the North is increased.
Northeast in the East is decreased.
Southeast in the East is decreased.
Southeast in the South is increased.
Southwest in the South is increased.
Southwest in the West is decreased.
Northwest in the West is decreased.
Northwest in the North is increased.

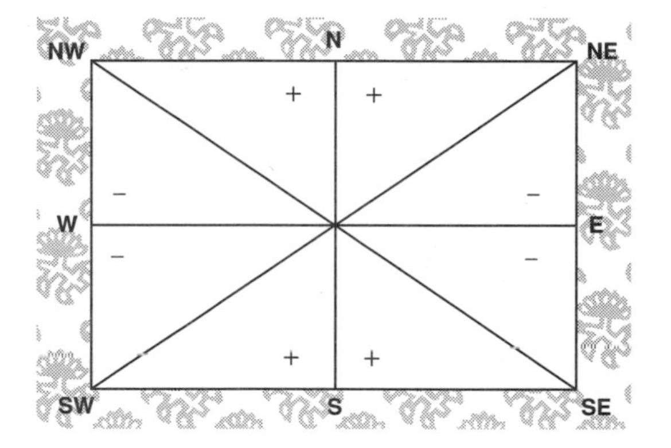

Fig. 19: Rectangle set in East–West direction

The opposite of the above takes place when the rectangle is set in North–South direction (fig. 20).

Northeast in the North is decreased.
Northeast in the East is increased.
Southeast in the South is decreased.
Southeast in the East is increased.
Southwest in the South is decreased.
Southwest in the West is increased.
Northwest in the West is increased.
Northwest in the North is decreased.

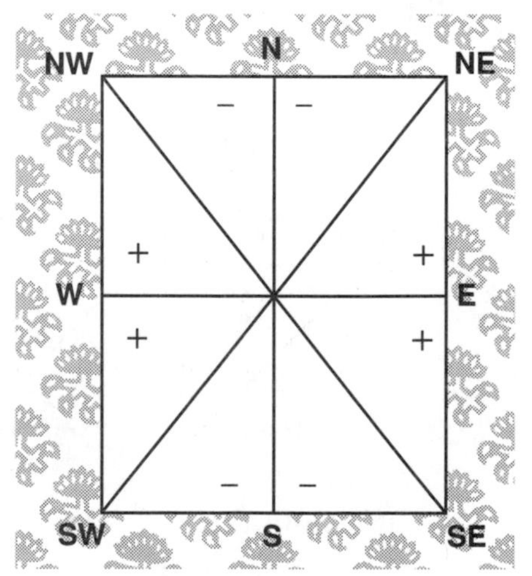

Fig. 20: Rectangle set in North-South direction

If the area under consideration is rotated less than 45 degrees (fig. 21), a line is drawn through the midpoint in the North–South direction. This line is then bisected in the East–West direction. Then lines are drawn through the center point, dividing each section into two at 45 degrees. This clearly delineates the exalted and debilitated positions.

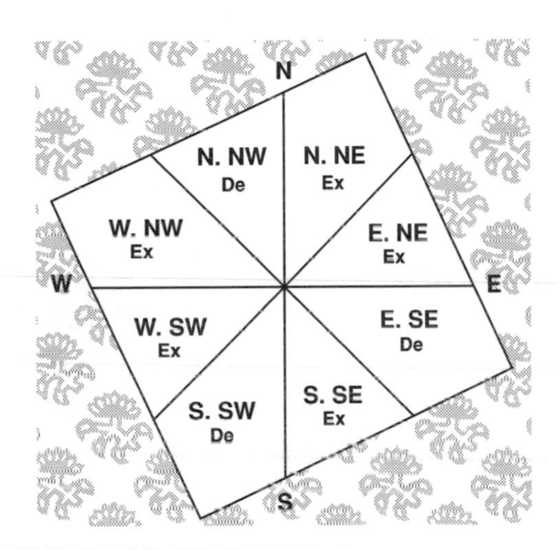

Fig. 21: Square rotated less than 45 degrees

To establish the exalted and debilitated positions in an area that is rotated 45 degrees, it is divided into eight sections, making sure all of the lines cross at the midpoint, as shown in figure 22.

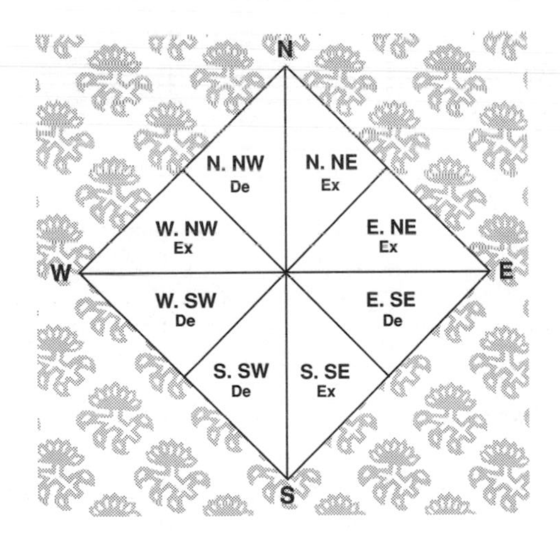

Fig. 22: Square rotated 45 degrees

Positive and Negative Energy Distribution

The concept of the basic principles of vaastu fits well into a theory of positive (beneficial) and negative (malefic) energy distribution. An open space, well, or water body seems to enhance the energy of a space, whether it is positive or negative. Similarly, a closed space or heavy weight seems to reduce the energy of a space, whether it is positive or negative. Although this understanding is not spelled out clearly in ancient vaastu texts, it seems to be an operative principle.

Thus, the positive energy of the Northeast is enhanced by keeping it lighter, with more open space, and with a downward slope toward the East and the North. Having wells, ponds, and lakes in that direction will also bring auspicious results. On the other hand, vaastu recommends more height and weight in the Southwest to reduce the negative energy that is concentrated there.

As we move to the Southeast and the Northwest, more neutral ground is established. The energies from the Southwest and Northeast meet at the Northwest and Southeast corners, establishing a neutrality (fig. 23). A space with pure energy that has no charge is established in the center. It represents the ether principle and is described in texts as *Brahmasthana* or the site of *brahman*, unmanifested universal consciousness.

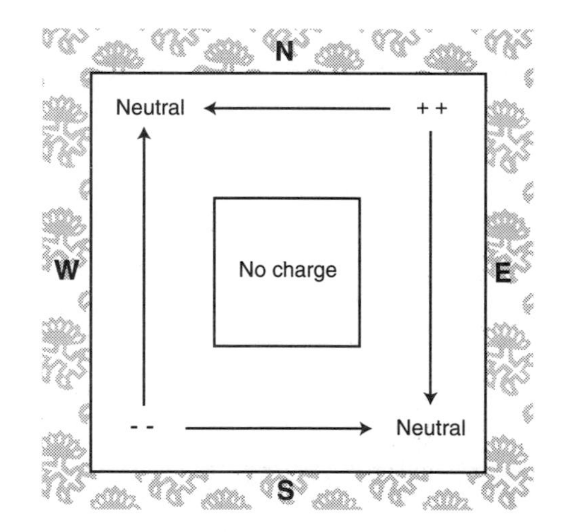

Fig. 23: The energy flow within a square

PART TWO

APPLYING VAASTU PRINCIPLES TO YOUR HOME

CHAPTER 6

THE RELATIONSHIP OF VAASTU TO YANTRA, MANTRA, AND TANTRA

The Unseen grew visible to student eyes,
Explained was the immense Inconscient's scheme,
Audacious lines were traced upon the Void;
The Infinite was reduced to square and cube.
Arranging symbol and significance,
Tracing the curve of a transcendent Power,
They framed the cabbala of the cosmic Law.
The balancing line discovered of Life's technique
And structured her magic and her mystery.

—Sri Aurobindo, *Savitri*

YANTRA IS A TOOL OR A SYMBOL conceived as a form pattern used to represent a deity or a cosmic principle. *Mantra* is the sound body of the principle. Upon constant repetition of a thought in the form of a mantra, the yantra is energized with the intended power of the mantra. When this energized yantra is used to accomplish a particular outcome, the process becomes known as *tantra.* In its highest essence tantra, the act, is the practice of the precept that the devotee with name and form is one in identity with the deity that is nameless and formless.

Yantra is used in different forms in all cultures and societies. Christians use the holy cross to worship Christ, the Islamic religion uses the crescent moon, Hinduism and Buddhism use many different yantras for various deities and planets. The logo a corporation uses to represent a theme or a vision is a yantra, though in its weakest sense, as is a country's flag.

Vedic seers used not only geometric patterns but also numbers, characters of the Sanskrit alphabet, and petals of the lotus flower in designing yantras. Vaastu directs the design and construction of a structure according to the correct arrangement and placement of the five elemental principles in such a way that the building itself acts as a yantra.

The yantras of the nine planets *(navagraha yantra)* are the main basis for vaastu design. Figures 24–32 illustrate the nine planetary yantras representing the nine planets considered by vedic astrology—Sun, Moon, Mars, Mercury, Jupiter, Venus, Saturn, Rahu (North Lunar Node), and Ketu (South Lunar Node). Each yantra is composed of nine squares. Each square is given a particular number to represent a particular planet. The middle square in the front row is given the number of the planet the yantra represents. The rest of the numbers follow according to a particular set pattern, so that the numbers of the three squares added either across or diagonally will equal the same total.

The principle of energy movement between planets provides further insight into how the exalted and debilitated positions came to be determined. Figure 33 shows the movement of energy between the planets depicted in the solar yantra.

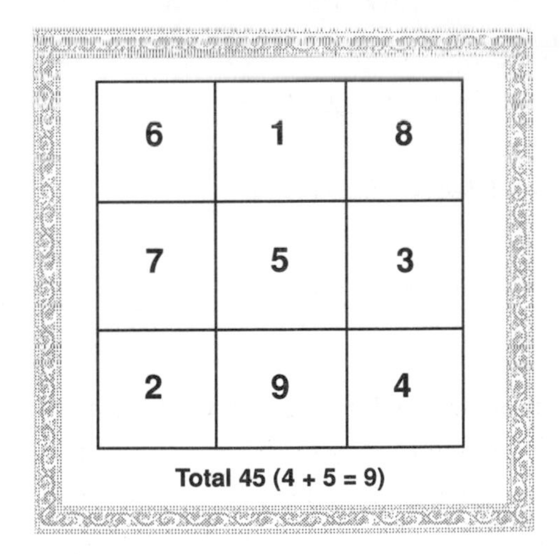

Fig. 24: Solar Yantra

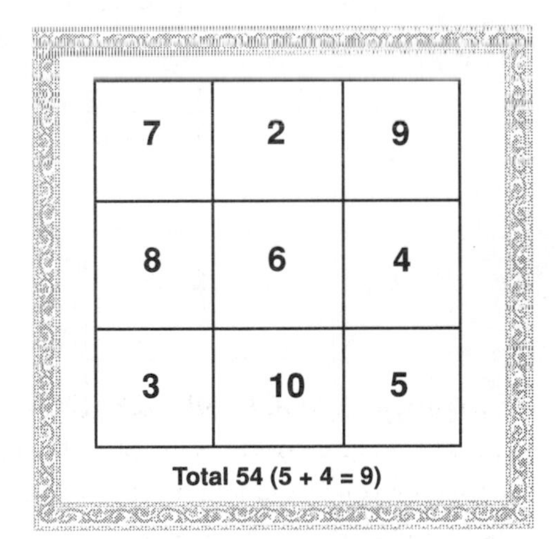

Fig. 25: Lunar Yantra

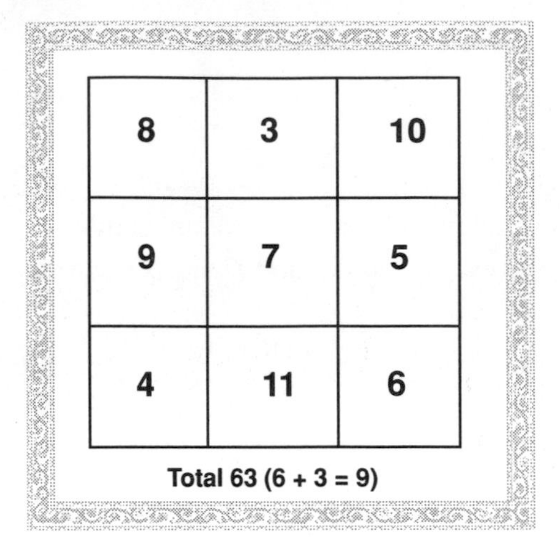

8	3	10
9	7	5
4	11	6

Total 63 (6 + 3 = 9)

Fig. 26: Mars Yantra

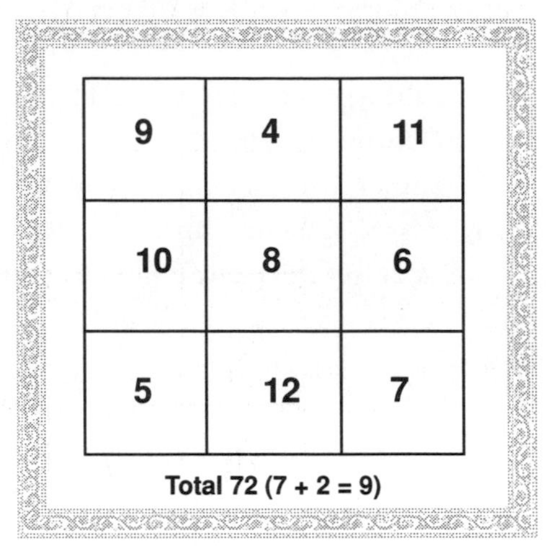

9	4	11
10	8	6
5	12	7

Total 72 (7 + 2 = 9)

Fig. 27: Mercury Yantra

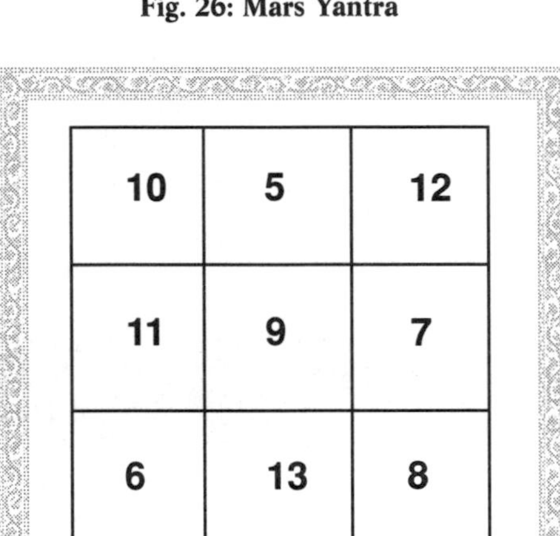

10	5	12
11	9	7
6	13	8

Total 81 (8 + 1 = 9)

Fig. 28: Jupiter Yantra

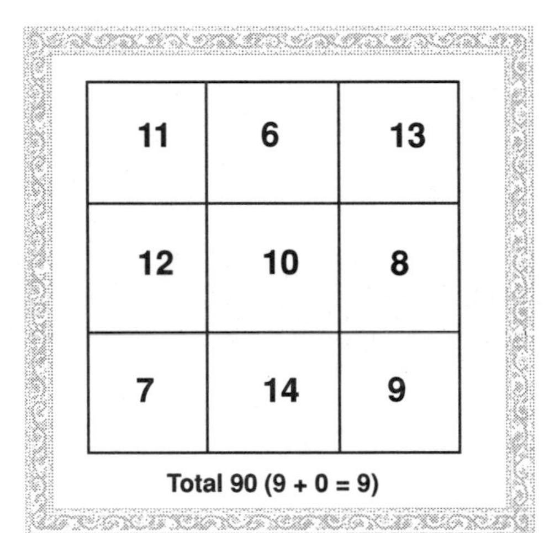

11	6	13
12	10	8
7	14	9

Total 90 (9 + 0 = 9)

Fig. 29: Venus Yantra

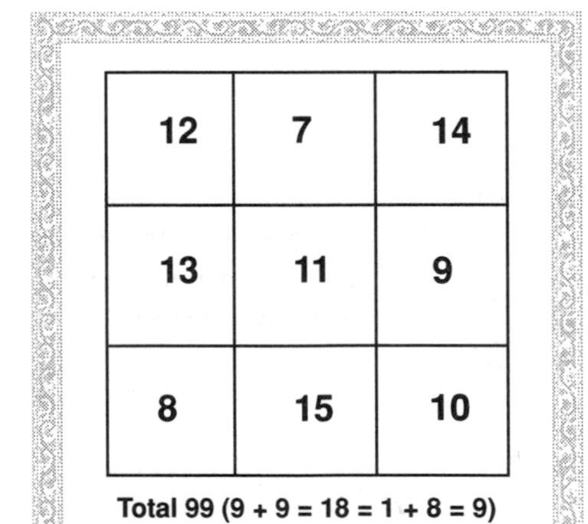

12	7	14
13	11	9
8	15	10

Total 99 (9 + 9 = 18 = 1 + 8 = 9)

Fig. 30: Saturn Yantra

13	8	15
14	12	10
9	16	11

Total 108 (1 + 8 = 9)

Fig. 31: Rahu Yantra

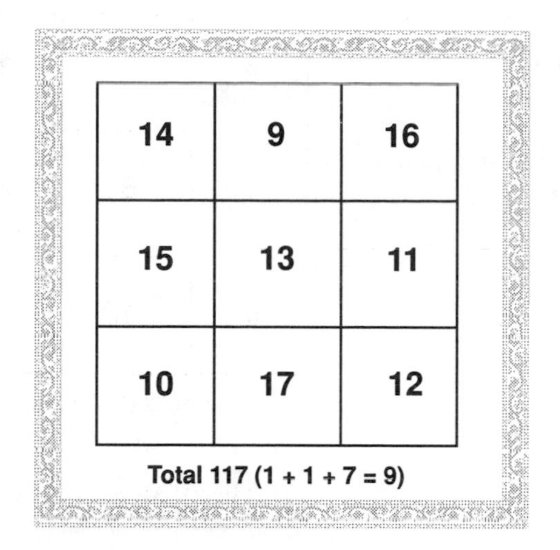

14	9	16
15	13	11
10	17	12

Total 117 (1 + 1 + 7 = 9)

Fig. 32: Ketu Yantra

The energy moves in through the Northern Northeast, Eastern Northeast, Southern Southeast, and Western Northwest. Energy moves out through the Southern Southwest, Western Southwest, Eastern Southeast, and Northern Northwest. It is very logical that the areas where energy is moving in should be regarded as exalted and should be the location of doors and windows, which provide openings for energy to flow in. Similarly, the areas where energy moves out are designated as debilitated and should be kept closed in order to prevent the loss of energy. The opposite of this situation—such as a wall in an exalted position and a door in a debilitated position—would cause negative effects by draining positive energy from the building.

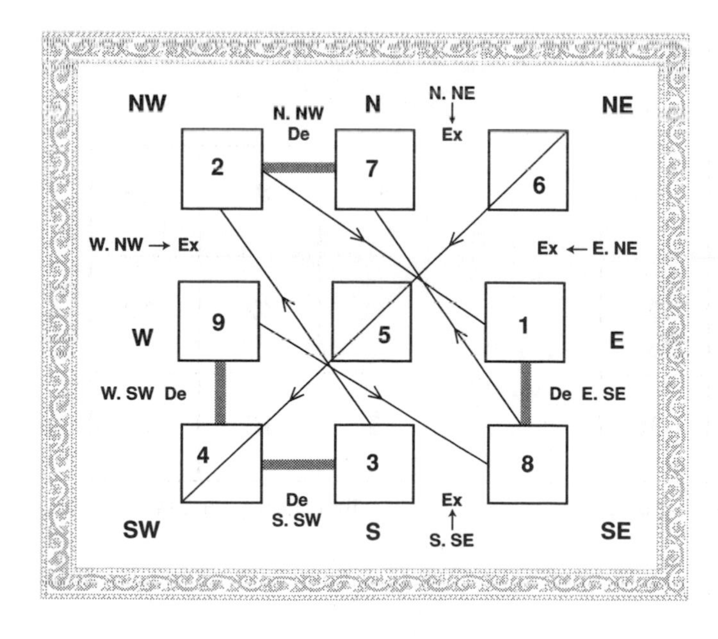

Fig. 33: Energy flow between planets and exalted and debilitated positions

THE SWASTIKA AND OTHER SYMBOLS

The swastika (fig. 34) has a great significance in vaastu. It is a modified version of the solar planetary yantra, as shown in figure 35.

Fig. 34: Swastika

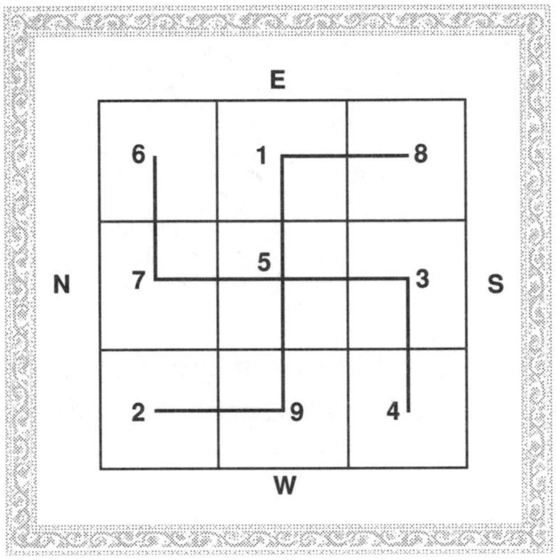

Fig. 35: Swastika and the solar yantra

The swastika is a symbol of peace and prosperity and brings good fortune and harmony to the inhabitants when placed in the front of a house. Whenever a powerful yantra is worshiped, it gives positive results and, conversely, if it is abused, it brings negative results. This appears to be the case in Adolf Hitler's choice of selecting the swastika symbol and rotating it by 45 degrees, as shown in figure 36. Six negative features result: energy is blocked in the otherwise exalted positions of Eastern Northeast and Southern Southeast; energy flows in from two debilitated positions, Southern Southwest and Eastern Southeast; and the otherwise exalted positions of Northern Northeast and Western Northwest become neutral points of no energy movement.

In vedic culture, worshiping a swastika is the same as worshiping a planetary yantra or the nine planets depicted as deities in many temples. Worship is given in the form of prayer *(navagraha pooja),* repetition of mantras *(japa),* and fire offerings *(homas).* These types of worship are known to ward off negative energy and bring in more positive energy. The proper display of symbols in the home has a similar effect. In particular, designs on the front door play an important role in vaastu. It is customary to use an auspicious symbol such as a swastika, a carving of OM, or a deity such as Lakshmi (the goddess of wealth) or Ganesha (the deity who removes

Fig. 36: The effect of rotation of swastika on energy flow

all obstacles). The use of symbols in our homes, guided by the precepts of vaastu, thus helps us to live a holistic life, in harmony with our immediate surroundings and ultimately with the energy flow of the whole universe.

CHAPTER 7

INTERIOR DESIGN

JUST AS A BEAUTIFUL PERSON of peaceful, harmonious nature attracts others and makes them feel happy, a house decorated according to vaastu principles will naturally make both inhabitants and guests feel an overall sense of well-being. When the principles of vaastu—such as height and weight and the locations of the five basic elements, planets, and deities—are applied to interior design, a house becomes like the expression of the divine nature itself. The incorporation of vaastu in the decoration of your home is fun and offers a rewarding process of becoming more aware of yourself and your surroundings. An individual is like a piezoelectric crystal in a radio. When the radio is properly tuned to a particular station, the crystal vibrates with the same frequency as the broadcasting frequency. The ancient sages tuned themselves to the harmony of the universe and derived the science of vaastu. Similarly, when you use the principles of vaastu to start observing nature more closely, you will become more aware of the effects of the subtle energies operating within and around you. Using vaastu in decorating your home will enable you to enhance the flow of natural harmony in your house, bringing positive energy to yourself and your guests.

Using vaastu to guide your choices of colors, materials, textures, furniture, and arrangements will enable you to decorate your house very tastefully. The five basic elements—ether, air, fire, water, and earth—and their governing locations form the background for your designing. The various planets and deities who govern different directions also guide the selection of colors and combinations of colors. Figures 37–40 show the positions of various governing elements and planets and the colors that correspond with them.

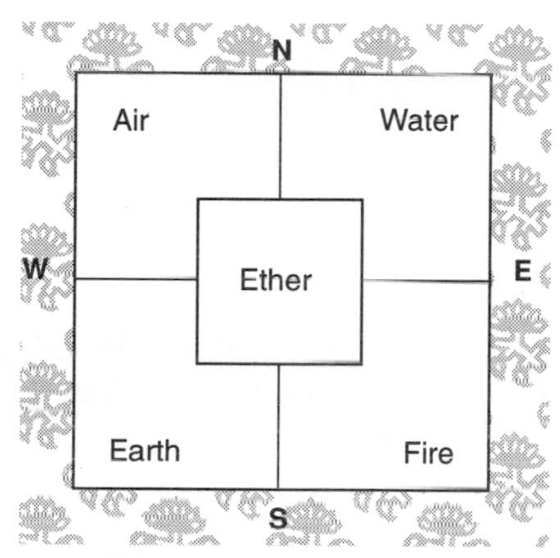

Fig. 37: Governing elements

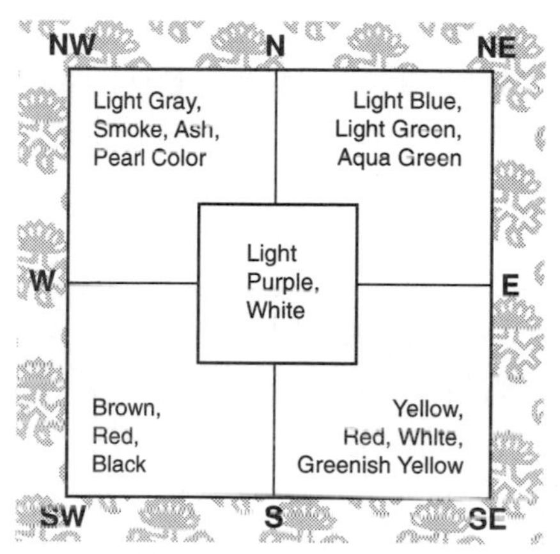

Fig. 38: Colors for each

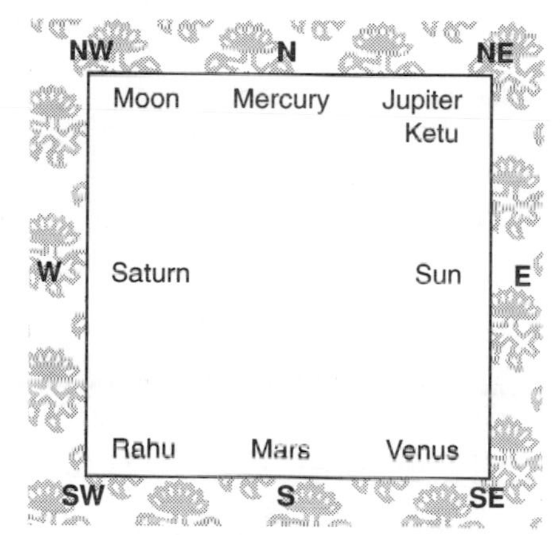

Fig. 39: Governing planets

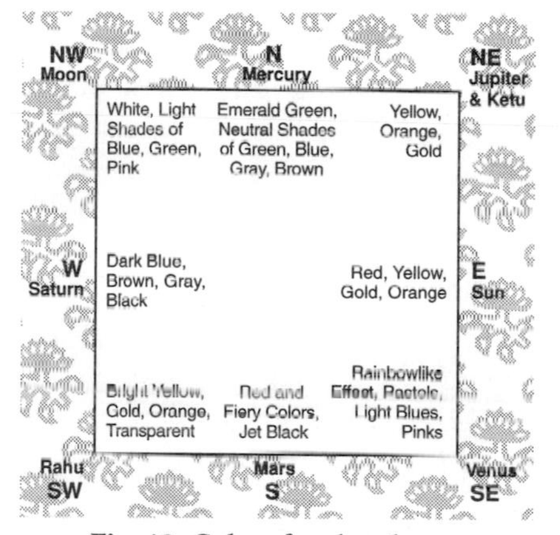

Fig. 40: Colors for the planets

Since both planets and elements can guide your choices, you have many color options for walls, floors, and fabrics. You can bring many colors or combinations of colors into the house, guided by your own good judgment and the following list, which identifies positive and negative choices for each area as indicated by the planet diagrams above.

1. Sun (East): Light, bright, clear. Warm colors such as red, yellow, gold, and orange.
2. Venus (Southeast): All colors. A rainbowlike effect, pastels, light blues,

pinks, light flowery variegated colors. Avoid dark and heavy colors, which are too bright and penetrating.

3. Mars (South): Red and fiery colors, darker hues and opaque tones, pure or jet black. Avoid gray, brown, blue, green, and very transparent bright colors like yellow.
4. Rahu (Southwest): Colors very similar to those of Jupiter and Sun. Bright yellow, gold, orange, and transparent.
5. Saturn (West): Dark blue, brown, gray, and black. But don't use in excess—they will strengthen the negative effects of Saturn. Blend with lighter shades of blue, brown, or black.
6. Moon (Northwest): White, light and somewhat bright shades of other colors such as blue, green, and pink. Avoid dark and cloudy colors, particularly dark gray and black.
7. Mercury (North): Use emerald green or neutral shades of green, blue, gray, and brown. Avoid red, orange, and dark colors.
8. Jupiter (Northeast): Use yellow, orange, and gold; clear, bright, and transparent colors. Avoid dark colors and strong shades like red, blue, violet, and purple.
9. Ketu (Northeast): Colors are like those for Sun. Red, orange, and yellow; bright, fiery, penetrating, and transparent. Avoid opaque or whitish-tinged colors as well as dark or cloudy colors.

The elemental principles should also be used to guide your selection of furniture materials and fabrics (fig. 41).

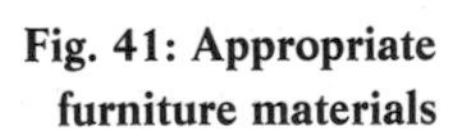

Fig. 41: Appropriate furniture materials

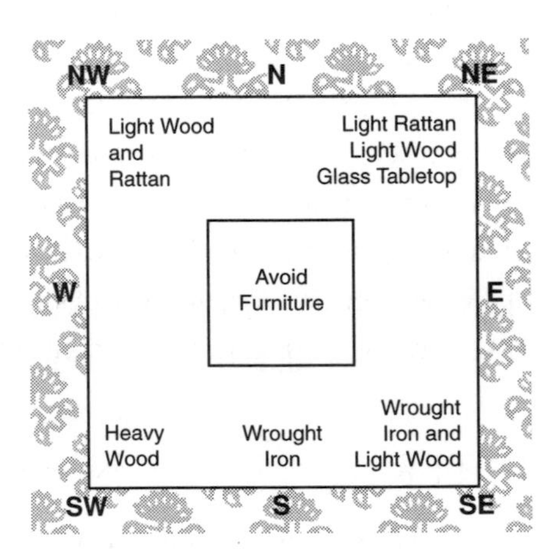

Southeast: Wrought iron and lighter kinds of wood
South: Wrought iron
Southwest: Heavy wood

Northwest: Light wood and rattan
Northeast: Light rattan, light wood, glass tabletops
For North, East, and West use combinations of the adjoining directions.

Pictures, photographs, and other wall decorations should be pleasant, proportionate to the area, and evocative of pleasant memories and feelings, such as nature scenes, themes of your religion, and family pictures. Try to coordinate the colors and frame material to the elements and planets.

The placement of both wall hangings and furniture in a room should also be guided by the principle of height and weight, as shown in figure 42.

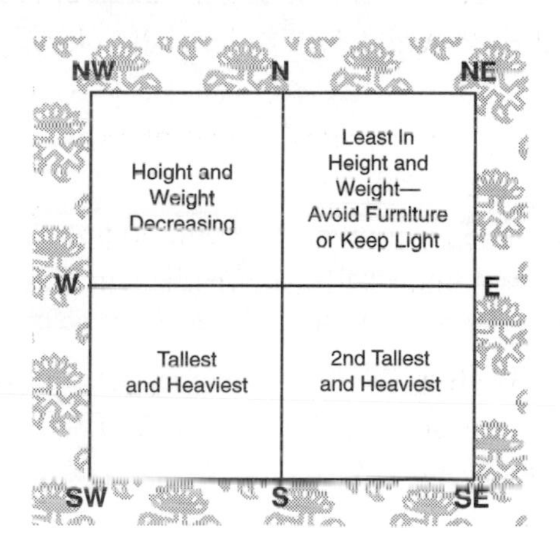

Fig. 42: Height and weight distribution

Figures 43 and 44 show typical vaastu layouts for a bedroom and a family room or living room. The first figure includes some of the common items that are used in a bedroom. Some alternate locations are also shown for different pieces of furniture. If the bed or any piece of furniture has to be placed near the Eastern or Northern wall, allow three to four inches of space between the wall and the furniture. In no case should the bed be placed on the North wall so that the head faces North.

This is a general outline for furniture placement. Taking your personal situation into account, try to arrange your furniture to conform to the height and weight principle.

INTERIOR DESIGN AS A HEALING ART

The knowledge of astrology (jyotish) can be combined with that of vaastu to further enhance the beneficial effects of both. If you know the details of the birth chart of a person and know which planets in the chart are benefic and malefic, you can enhance the benefic energies through proper color selections in the environment.

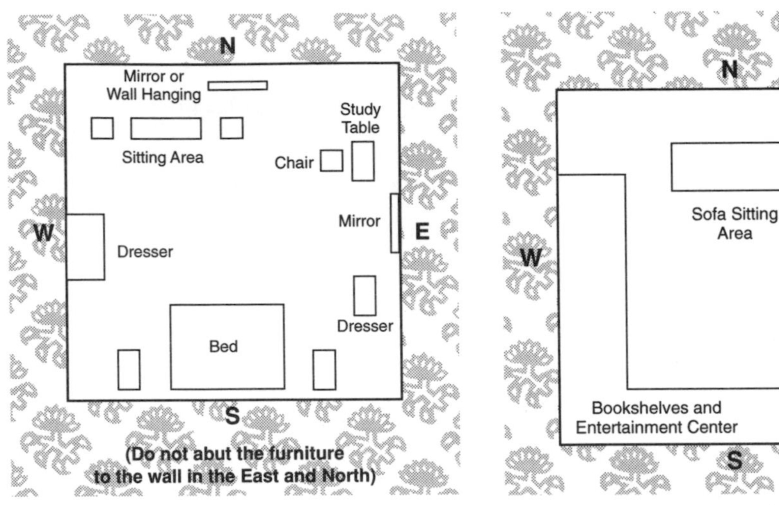

Fig. 43: Bedroom

Fig. 44: Family and living room

Similarly, you can reduce the energy of malefic planets. Light and neutral colors should be used where planetary energies are negative to the person, and stronger, brighter colors should be used when a planetary position is weak in the chart. Both can be accomplished by following this rule of thumb:

Use lighter colors with small accents of darker colors for malefic planets—Saturn, Mars, Rahu, Ketu, and Sun.

For all benefic planets—Jupiter, Venus, Moon, and Mercury—that are exalted, use lighter colors with brighter colors as accents.

For all benefic planets—Jupiter, Venus, Moon, and Mercury—that are in weak positions, use brighter colors with light colors as accents.

Planetary energies are closely related to a person's moods and physical and psychological well-being. Thus, once you have understood the principles of interior design according to vaastu, you can use this knowledge to benefit others as well as yourself. Knowledge of astrology and ayurveda, combined with the mastery of vaastu, is a wonderful tool that can be used to help people in many ways. If a person is suffering from a particular health ailment, it is possible to use their birth chart and ayurvedic diagnosis to design color combinations that can be truly healing. Even in situations where the person may not be interested in this science or believe in it, these principles can be compassionately applied to effect healing without his or her knowledge. Colors and textures of fabric and furniture can be combined in subtle ways to harmonize the planetary and elementary energies in and around a house and bring health and well-being to the inhabitants.

CHAPTER 8
LANDSCAPING

Mother Nature

Live in complete harmony with Nature,
Experience the grace of God in the
Splendor of the universe.
Be blessed by God's reassuring love,
The sweet dawn will sweeten your soul,
The dazzling mid-day will set your
Hearts aflutter.
And the serene music of your soul will
Guide you towards peace and prosperity.
And when the day's task is over you
will sleep in the lap of Mother Nature,
All the deities will be favorable to you.

—Rig Veda

GREAT IMPORTANCE IS GIVEN to landscaping in ancient vaastu texts, where it is referred to as pleasure gardens. The topics covered include: the planting of trees; the importance of the spatial directions; groundwater; exhaustive details on how to prepare soil; and seeds for germination and planting. There are very strict rules and regulations for both the planting and cutting of trees. Various auspicious times *(muhoortas)* are recommended for these actions based on the individual's birth star and the governing star and deity of the plants. The *Brihat Samhita* dwells on these matters quite extensively. Surapala's *Vrikshayurveda* is another ancient text that, though lost, is often quoted. It has recently been recovered and translated into

English. Another classical text is *Sarangadharapaddati* by Sarangadhara of the thirteenth century. It describes details of planting, soil preparation, pest control, various types of nourishing manure, and even water divination in the chapter titled "Upavanavinoda."

Landscaping in vaastu is guided by the knowledge of the directions, the nature of various planetary forces, and their effects on the elements. Like interior design according to vaastu, it seeks to balance these forces, as well as taking into consideration the *tridhaatu (vaata, pitta, kapha)* constitution of plants. The fundamental principle of ayurveda is that *vaata, pitta,* and *kapha* should be in balance for health and longevity. Ancient wisdom taught that humans and the plant kingdom were both governed by the same principles of cosmic consciousness, which manifest in diverse ways, operating in all animate and inanimate objects in different proportions. This is the basis for using herbs as medicine in ayurvedic practice. *Vaata* governs movement such as circulation, breathing, and excretion. *Pitta* governs all the metabolic activities such as digestion, absorption, and assimilation. *Kapha* acts as the binding that holds cells together in a growing organism. The parallel activities in plants are photosynthesis, absorption of nutrients from the soil, and growth. Vedic literature is thus rich in details of various medicinal plants and their *tridhaatu* constitution, as well as copious details on their presiding planets, deities, and stars.

Figure 45 shows the distribution of the *tridhaatu* principle in a piece of property. The *dhaatus (vaata, pitta, and kapha)* merge into each other gradually at their meeting points. Plants that have parallel combinations of the *dhaatus* can be planted in those areas. The location of flowering plants in areas where the *dhaatus* are equal can be selected based on planetary colors as shown in the preceding chapter, "Interior Design."

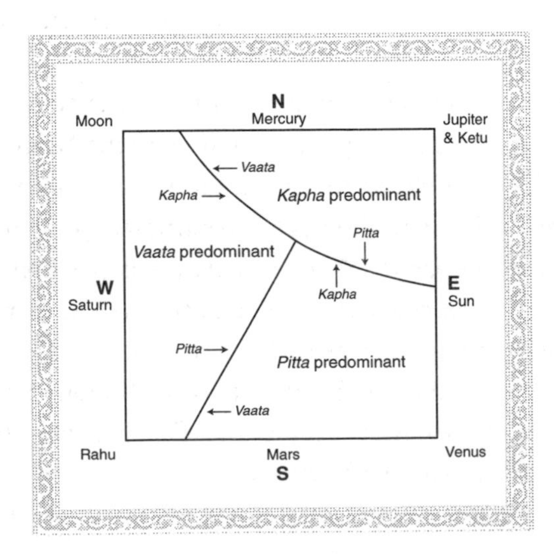

Fig. 45: The *tridhaatu* composition of a piece of property

The deep intuition of the ancient vaastu sages went beyond the ordinary physical plane of matter to subtler energy levels, revealing that nature is interlinked and no item can be separated from the one cosmic consciousness—named *virat* (all inclusive)—which is the basis of the quantum soup that makes this whole universe. They were aware of various interconnections between the subtle essences of plants and planetary forces. Thus, vaastu gives explanations as to the consequences of planting different plants in right and wrong directions. The interrelationships between various plants and their synergistic and antagonistic properties are also explained. The vast knowledge of plants contained in vaastu will enable one to create a landscape that is not only aesthetically pleasing but also perfectly balanced to foster peace and well-being.

The information on vaastu landscaping is very exhaustive and beyond the scope of this book. However, I have given below an outline of the general principles and several charts illustrating the correspondences between plants, planets, *dhaatus,* and directions. For more detailed guidance, the reader may consult the references mentioned above.

GENERAL VAASTU PRINCIPLES FOR LANDSCAPING

1. Ground Preparation: Make sure that the ground to the North and East is not elevated above the house foundation. The ground on the South and West sides can be higher than the foundation level or at the same level all around, but not lower than the level of the ground to the East or North.
2. Ponds and other water bodies should be in the Northeast sector.
3. If you are creating a stream, it should flow toward the North or East.
4. If you are creating a waterfall, it should be on the Southeast side, flowing toward the North.
5. Rocks and rock formations should be on the South or West side.
6. A children's play area, such as a swing set, should be in the Northwest.
7. Whenever possible, plants should be selected carefully to balance the *vaata, pitta,* and *kapha* principles. For aesthetic purposes, you may wish to include ornamental plants for which the *tridhaatu* composition is not known. In that case, try to coordinate the color of the flowers or plants with the colors of the governing planets for each direction.
8. All tall trees should be planted in the South and West. No tall tree should be planted in the North or East in such a way that the shadow of the tree falls on the house for more than two hours a day.
9. The Southwest and Northeast corners should be kept free of any trees.

10. No milk-sap–yielding plant should be in the garden.
11. No thorny plants should be placed on the East or North side.
12. The Southwest and Northeast corners should be kept free of plants, except Bilva *(Aegle marmelos)* in the Southwest.
13. Aromatic plants are more potent than nonaromatic plants. Following the guidelines above and in the charts below, try to include one or two aromatic plants in each direction.
14. Most medicinal plants are not ornamental plants and thus are not very suitable for aesthetic landscaping. However, they can be included if the other guidelines are followed.

The following plants are grouped according to the *tridhaatu* zone where they should be planted.

Plants for Vaata Zone

VAATA–BALANCING

1. Cinnamon Basil *(O.Basilicum)*
2. Bugloss, Viper's *(Echium Vulgare)*
3. Caraway *(Carum carvi)*
4. Cumin *(Cuminum cyminum)*
5. Evening Primrose *(O enothera biennis)*
6. Indian Dill *(Anethum Sowa)*
7. Sweet Fennel *(Foeniculum Vulgare)*
8. Tila (Sesame oil) *(Sesamum indicum)*
9. Palandu (Onion) *(Allium cepa)*
10. Kushmanda (Sweet Pumpkin) *(Benincasa hispida)*
11. Eranda *(Ricinus comnunis)*

Plants for Pitta Zone

PITTA–BALANCING

1. Arjuna *(Terminalia arjuna)*
2. Karpura-Camphor *(Cinnamomum camphora)*
3. Lemon Basil *(Ocimum Americanum)*
4. Cardamom *(Elettaria cardamomum)*
5. Daisy, English *(Dellis perennis)*
6. Dandelion, French *(Taraxacum officinale)*
7. Dead Nettle, Purple *(Laniium pupureum)*
8. Slippery Elm *(Ulmus rubra)*

9. Echinacea (*Echinacea purpurea)*
10. Ground Ivy (*Glechoma hederancea)*
11. Jathi (*Jasminum officinale linn)*

Plants for Kapha Zone

KAPHA–(BALANCING)

1. Cinnamon (*Cinnamomum Zeylanicum)*
2. Red Clover (*Trifolium pratense)*
3. Daisy, Oxeye (*Chrysanthemum leucanthemum)*
4. Elecampane (*Inula helenium)*
5. Ginger (*Zingziber officinale)*
6. Manduka parni (*Centella asiatica)*
7. Jyothishmathi (*Celastrus paniculatus)*
8. Vacha (*Acorus calamus)*
9. Rasona (Garlic) (*Allium sativum)*
10. Sarshapa (*Brassica campestris)*
11. Chakramarda (*Cassia tora)*

CORRESPONDENCES BETWEEN PLANTS, PLANETS, ZODIAC SIGNS, AND STARS

The tables below give detailed information about various plants and their connections to different deities, planets, zodiac signs, and stars. Although the lists are quite long, they can easily be used to design a garden around your home that will bring peace of mind and prosperity to its inhabitants. Simply choose a few plants for each direction, following the general guidelines given above and the *dhaltu* areas as mapped out on figure 45.

PLANET	LATIN PLANT NAME	VEDIC PLANT NAME
Sun	*Calotropis procera*	Arka
Moon	*Butea monosperma*	Palasha
Mars	*Acacia catechu*	Khadira
Mercury	*Achyranthes aspera*	Apamarga
Jupiter	*Ficus religiosa*	Ashwatha
Venus	*Ficus racemosa*	Udumbara
Saturn	*Acacia ferrogenia*	Shami
Rahu	*Cynodon dactylon*	Durva
Ketu	*Desmostachya bipinnata*	Darbha

ZODIAC SIGN	LATIN PLANT NAME	VEDIC PLANT NAME
Aries (Mesha)	*Phyllanthus emblica*	Amalaki
Taurus (Vrishabha)	*Acacia catechu*	Khadhira
Gemini (Mithuna)	*Acacia ferrugenea*	Shami
Cancer (Karkataka)	*Bambusa arundinacea*	Vamsha
Leo (Simha)	*Ficus microcarpa*	Plaksha
Virgo (Kanya)	*Aegle marmelos*	Bilva
Libra (Tula)	*Terminalia arjuna*	Arjuna
Scorpio (Vrischika)	*Mimusops elengi*	Bakula
Sagittarius (Dhanus)	*Artocarpus heterophyllus*	Panasa
Capricorn (Makara)	*Calotropis procera*	Arka
Aquarius (Kumbha)	*Enthocephallus kadamba*	Kadamba
Pisces (Meena)	*Mangifera indica*	Amra

STAR	LATIN PLANT NAME	VEDIC PLANT NAME
1. Ashvini	*Strychnos nux-vomica*	Kupilu
2. Bharani	*Phyllanthus emblica*	Amalaki
3. Krithika	*Ficus racemosa*	Udumbara
4. Rohini	*Syzygium cumini*	Jambu
5. Mrigashira	*Acacia catechu*	Khadira
6. Ardra	*Gmelina arborea*	Badraparni
7. Punaravasu	*Bambusa arundinacea*	Vamsha
8. Pushya	*Ficus religiosa*	Ashwatha
9. Aslesha	*Calophyllum inophyllum*	Punnaga
10. Makha	*Ficus benghalensis*	Vata
11. Pubba	*Butea monosperma*	Palasha
12. Uttara	*Ficus microcarpa*	Plaksha
13. Hasta	*Spondias mangifera*	Ambashta
14. Chitra	*Aegle marmelos*	Bilva
15. Swati	*Terminalia arjuna*	Arjuna
16. Vishaka	*Flacourtia indica*	Vikantaka
17. Anuradha	*Mimusops elengi*	Bakula
18. Jeshta	*Bombax ceiba*	Shalmali
19. Moola	*Santalum album*	Chandana
20. Purvashada	*Jagnivadol bengidia*	Krishna pulgha
21. Uttarashada	*Artocarpus heterophyllus*	Panasa
22. Sharavana	*Calotropis gigantea*	Arka

STAR	LATIN PLANT NAME	VEDIC PLANT NAME
23. Dhanishta	*Acacia ferrugenea*	Shami
24. Shatabhisha	*Enthocephallus kadamba*	Kadamba
25. Purvabhadra	*Azadirachta indica*	Nimba
26. Uttararabhadra	*Mangifera indica*	Amra
27. Revati	*Madhuca longifolia*	Madhuka

The following chart is a general list of medicinal plants recommended for general landscaping. This information could also be used to develop a large herbal garden for medicinal purposes, such as the one at our Indus Valley Ayurvedic Center in Mysore.

For the North Side:

1. *Ficus religiosa* (Ashwatha)—This tree should be planted in the Northern Northeast
2. *Syzygium cumini* (Jambu)
3. *Eclipta alba* (Bringaraja)
4. *Michelia champaca* (Champaka)
5. *Dolicos lablab* (Nishpavah)
6. *Jasminum auriculatum* (Suchimallika)
7. *Cymbopogon citratus* (Bhustrina)
8. *Vinca rosea* (Nityakalyam)
9. *Punica granatum* (Dadima)
10. *Nerium indicum* (Karavira)
11. *Sesbania grandiflora* (Agastya)
12. *Citrus limon* (Jambeera)
13. *Limonia acidissima* (Kapitta)
14. *Artocarpus heterophyllus* (Panasah)
15. *Ficus racemosa* (Udumbara)
16. *Aegle marmelos* (Bilva)—This tree should be planted in Northwest direction

For the East Side:

1. *Musa paradisiaca* (Kadali)
2. *Ananas comosus* (Ananasum)
3. *Colocasia esculenta* (Alukam)
4. *Zingiber officinale* (Shunti)
5. *Ocimum sanctum* (Tulasi)
6. *Nyctanthes arbor-tristis* (Parijatha)

7. *Saraca indica* (Ashoka)
8. *Anacardium Occidentale* (Vrikkabeeja)

For the South Side:

1. *Gossypium herbaceum* (Karpasa)
2. *Ricinus communis* (Eranda)
3. *Carica papaya* (Erandakarkati)
4. *Coccinia grandis* (Bimbi)
5. *Trachyspermum ammi* (Ajamoda)
6. *Azadirachta indica* (Nimba)
7. *Ruta chalepensis* (Nagadali)
8. *Tinospora cordifolia* (Amrutha)
9. *Rosa centifolia* (Shathapathra)
10. *Mangifera indica* (Ashoka)

For the Southwest Side:

1. *Anthocephallus kadamba* (Kadamba)
2. *Vitex negundo* (Nirgundi)
3. *Euphorbia ligularia* (Snuhi)
4. *Phyllanthus emblica* (Amalaki)
5. *Moringa oleifera* (Shigru)
6. *Mimusops elengi* (Bakula)
7. *Pongamia pinnata* (Karanja)

For the West Side:

1. *Jasminum grandiflorum* (Jati)
2. *Jasminum sambac* (Mallika)
3. *Plumeria rubra* (Shweta champaka)
4. *Lawsonia inermis* (Medhini)
5. *Albizzia lebbeck* (Sirisha)—This tree should be planted in Northwest corner

Note: The taller trees should be planted farther away from the house to avoid shadows falling on the house. If you have a small garden and this is not possible, then you should plant only on the South and West sides.

PART THREE

PROPERTY ASSESSMENT AND CORRECTION

CHAPTER 9

UNDERSTANDING EXTENSION

A GOOD QUALITY COMPASS IS ESSENTIAL to the study of vaastu. It should be sufficiently calibrated to give an accurate reading of the degrees. It is best to rest the compass on a steady platform away from any magnetic objects during a reading. To confirm that the reading is accurate, the compass should be moved to two or three different positions. One has to be especially careful while taking readings near metal, such as inside steel-reinforced concrete buildings or even near one's own belt buckle.

The ideal vaastu plot is a square that perfectly accommodates the body of Vaastupurusha. However, plots are often not an exact square or rectangle. When a plot has irregular sides or only one deviated side, the situation becomes very complex, but the following method for assessment is easy to use. An extension or cut in a plot in any direction is measured from the midpoint of that direction. Hold the compass facing North and stand on each side of the plot, noting whether the needle of the compass deviates either to the right or to the left. Figure 46 shows the results when the compass deviates to the right, and figure 47 shows the results when it deviates to the left.

In figure 46, the needle of the compass indicates that exact North is slightly to the right side of the direction of the plot, causing the following:

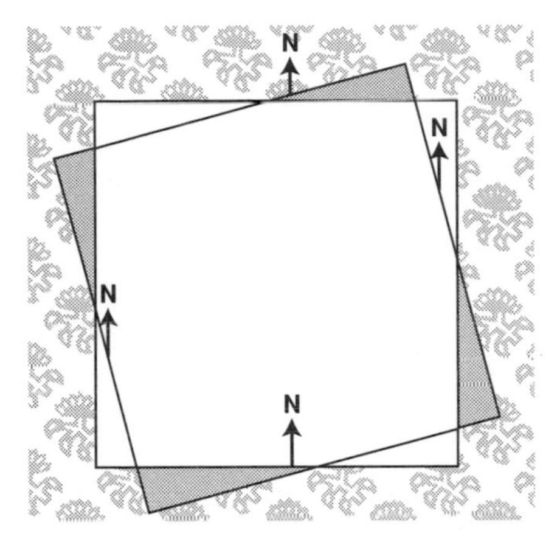

Fig. 46: Showing North to your right side (shaded area represents the plot)

Northern Northeast extension on the North side;
Eastern Southeast extension on the East side;
Southern Southwest extension on the South side;
Western Northwest extension on the West side.

Figure 47 describes the situation when the needle of the compass indicates that exact North is slightly to the left side of the direction of the plot, causing the following:

Northern Northwest extension on the North side;
Eastern Northeast extension on the East side;
Southern Southeast extension on the South side;
Western Southwest extension on the West side.

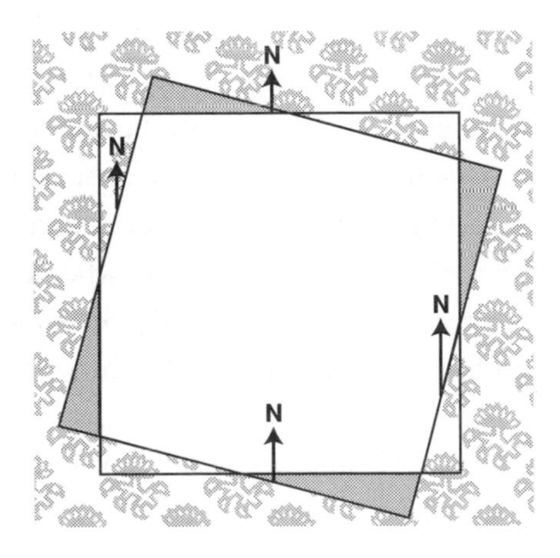

Fig. 47: Showing North to your left side (shaded area represents the plot)

The compass is a handy tool that provides a fairly accurate determination of the orientation of a piece of property. However, as one moves away from the equator toward the North or the South, the compass indication of North becomes increasingly inaccurate. In addition, Earth's polarity changes approximately every twenty-five thousand years, making previous compasses obsolete.

Vaastu does not change under these circumstances because it is not based on Earth's polarity. Instead, it is based on the Sun's position in relation to Earth. In vedic times, before the development of the magnetic compass, a different method—derived from the sun's shadow—was used to determine the directions. The classical text *Mayamata* describes this method as follows:

> Make an 18-inch-high post out of wood. It should be 4 inches square at the bottom and 1½ inches square at the top. This is known as a gnomon. Stand it vertically on a flat surface of the land whose orientation you wish to determine, as shown in figure 48.

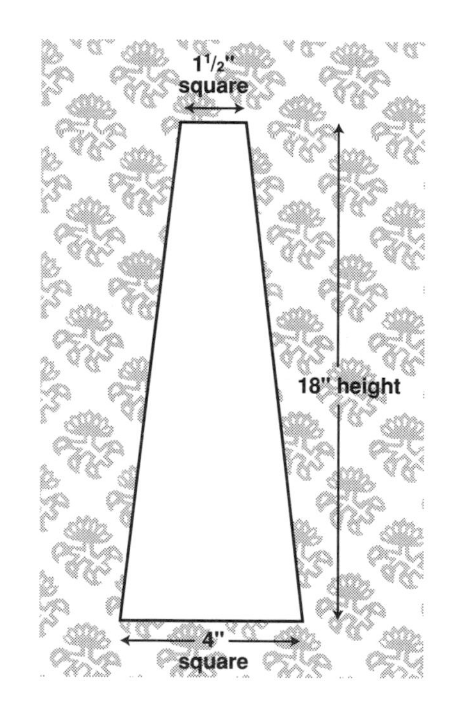

Fig. 48: Gnomon

> Draw a circle around it with a 36-inch radius.
>
> Observe and mark the two points on the edge of the circle where the shadow of the post touches the circle before noon and after noon. Draw a line joining these two points. Then draw a perpendicular line through

the midpoint of the line joining the two points, as shown in figure 49. The perpendicular line will indicate the correct North for that location, which will deviate several degrees from magnetic North.

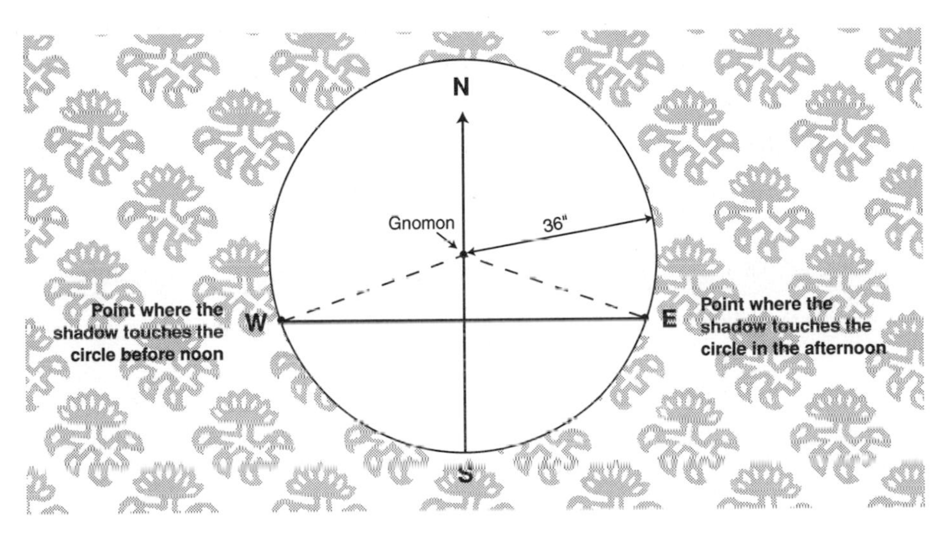

Fig. 49: How to mark the shadow

CHAPTER 10

EVALUATING EXTENSIONS AND CUTS

VAASTU IDENTIFIES SOME EXTENSIONS and cuts as acceptable and some as unacceptable, based on the theory of energy distribution, height and weight distribution, and governing planets and deities. Figures 50–65 illustrate each of the possible kinds of cuts and extensions and their influences.

Figure 50: Northern Northeast cut—not acceptable. It generally hinders progress as well as causing financial losses and other troubles to female children.

Figure 51: Northern Northeast extension—acceptable. It increases financial fortunes and brings good luck to female children. It fosters the ability of the occupants to spend money thriftily and create good financial reserves.

Figure 52: Eastern Northeast cut—not acceptable. It causes the lack of wisdom and prosperity. Male children will have problems.

Figure 53: Eastern Northeast extension—acceptable. It results in good prosperity and generosity.

Figure 54: Eastern Southeast cut—acceptable. However, the total weight of the plot and building must be correctly balanced during construction.

Figure 55: Eastern Southeast extension—not acceptable. It causes disputes in the family, as well as fire accidents and robbery.

**Fig. 50: Northern Northeast cut—
not acceptable**

**Fig. 51: Northern Northeast extension—
acceptable**

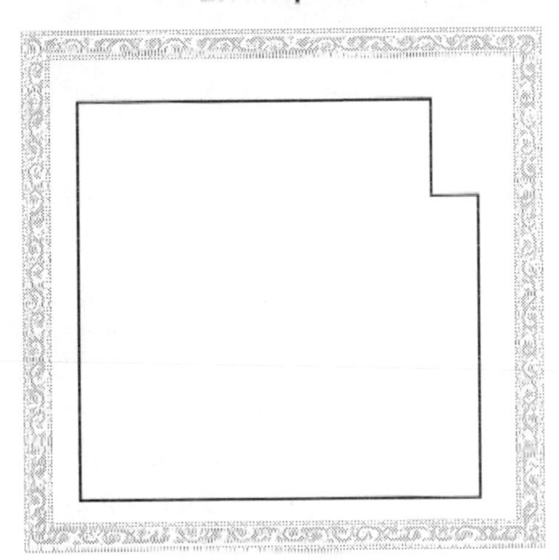

**Fig. 52: Eastern Northeast cut—
not acceptable**

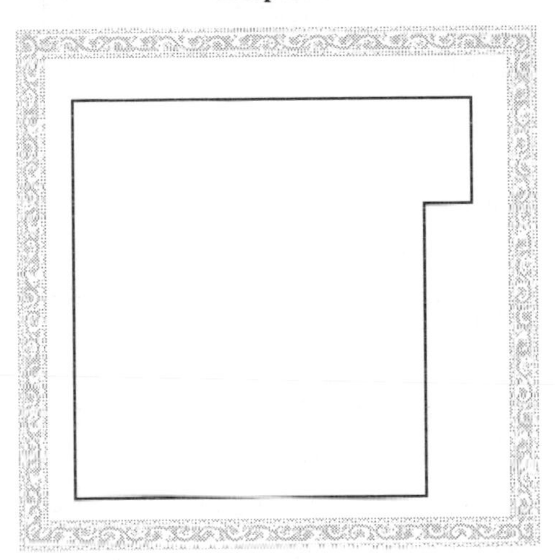

**Fig. 53: Eastern Northeast extension—
acceptable**

**Fig. 54: Eastern Southeast cut—
acceptable**

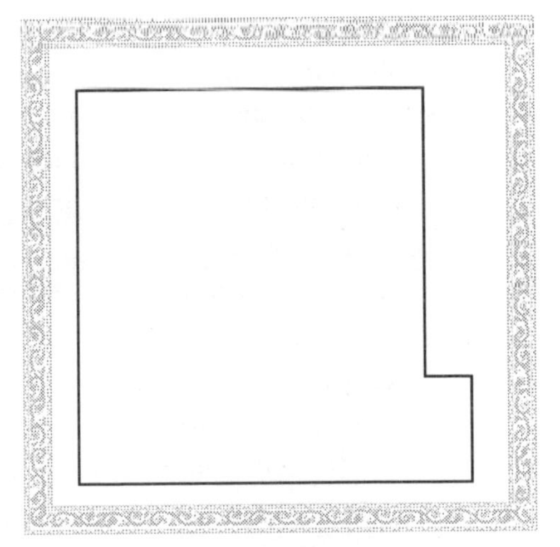

**Fig. 55: Eastern Southeast extension—
not acceptable**

Fig. 56: Southern Southeast cut—acceptable

Fig. 57: Southern Southeast extension—not acceptable

Fig. 58: Southern Southwest cut—acceptable

Fig. 59: Southern Southwest extension—not acceptable

Figure 56: Southern Southeast cut—acceptable. No untoward effects.

Figure 57: Southern Southeast extension—not acceptable. This brings ill effects to the second child, especially to the second female child. It can cause cancer in the family.

Figure 58: Southern Southwest cut—acceptable.

Figure 59: Southern Southwest extension—not acceptable. It increases the negative results of Southern Southwest, causing ill health, accidents, and financial loses. The female head of the family is most affected.

Fig. 60: Western Southwest cut—acceptable

Fig. 61: Western Southwest extension—not acceptable

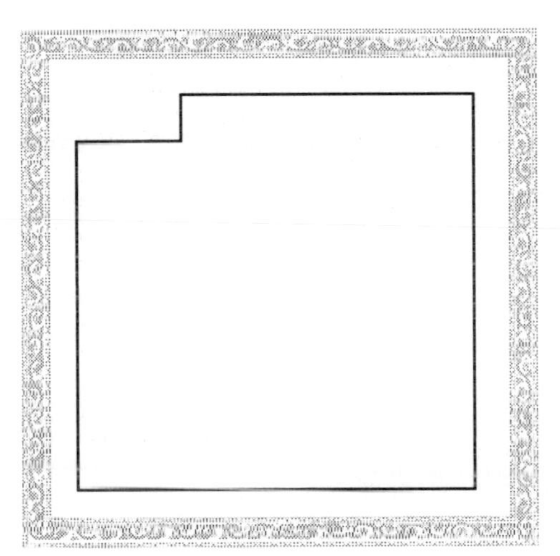

Fig. 62: Northern Northwest cut—acceptable

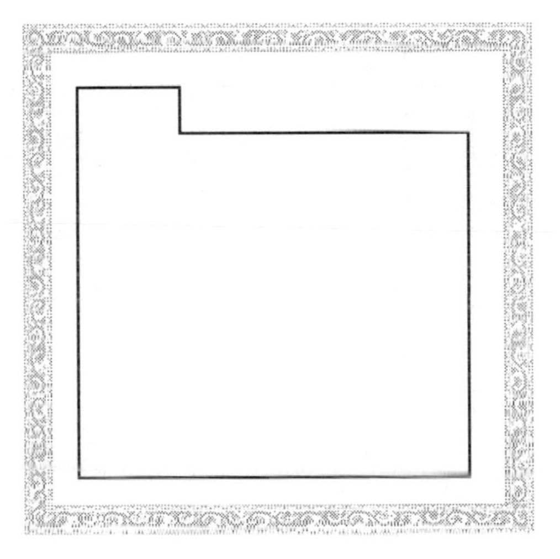

Fig. 63: Northern Northwest extension—not acceptable

Figure 60: Western Southwest cut—acceptable. No ill effects result.

Figure 61: Western Southwest extension—not acceptable. It brings ill health to the male head of the family.

Figure 62: Northern Northwest cut—acceptable. It does not cause any ill effects.

Figure 63: Northern Northwest extension—not acceptable. It causes bad character, financial losses, estrangement, and divorce.

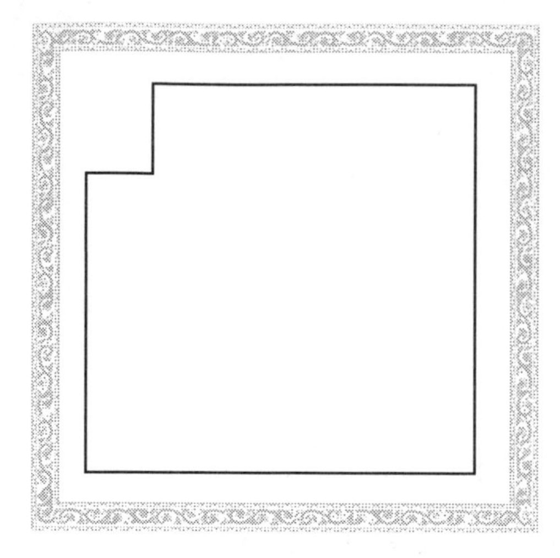

Fig. 64: Western Northwest cut—acceptable

Fig. 65: Western Northwest extension—not acceptable

Figure 64: Western Northwest cut—acceptable. No untoward effects come of in this situation.

Figure 65: Western Northwest extension—not acceptable. It causes an unwarranted bad reputation for the occupant.

CHAPTER 11

RECTIFICATION OF EXTENSIONS AND CUTS

RECTIFICATION IS REQUIRED when a plot is not set to square. In vaastu, the angles at the four corners are important. The Southwest corner must be set to 90 degrees exactly. If it is greater than 90 degrees, it will cause the extension of the Northwest or the Southeast. If it is less than 90 degrees, it will cause a cut in the Northwest or the Southeast. The Northwest and Southeast can be 90 degrees or greater but never less than 90 degrees as that causes a cut in the Northeast. The Northeast could be 90 degrees or less but never greater than 90 degrees. If it is less than 90 degrees, it creates a Northeastern extension. Figures 66–68 illustrate the extensions considered to be suitable by vaastu.

Some extensions and cuts can be corrected by abandoning small areas such as the segments shaded in figures 69–75. Abandonment of an area means that after determining the correction for any extension or cuts, the area to be deleted from your property should be sold or given to a charitable organization. When this is not possible, a compound wall should be built along the corrected border, and the excess piece of land should not be used by the owner for any purpose.

Figure 69: Southeast extension, both in the Southern Southeast and the Eastern Southeast, is suitable when corrected by the abandonment of the marked area.

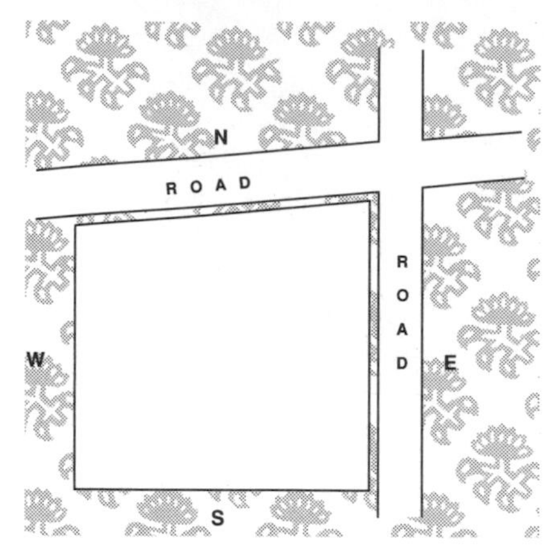

Fig. 66: Northeast extension—suitable

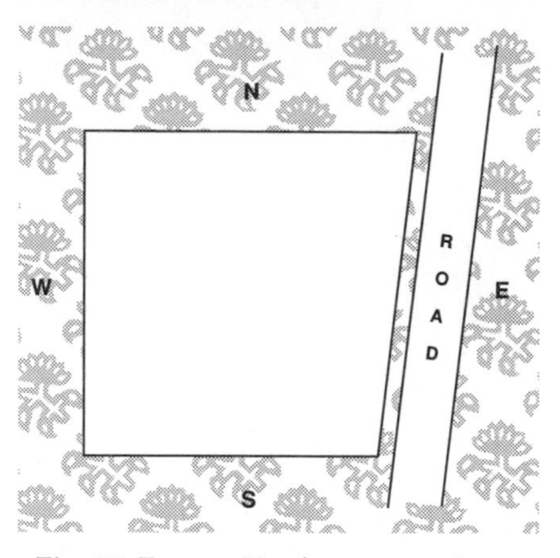

Fig. 67: Eastern Northeast extension—suitable

Fig. 68: Northern Northeast extension—suitable

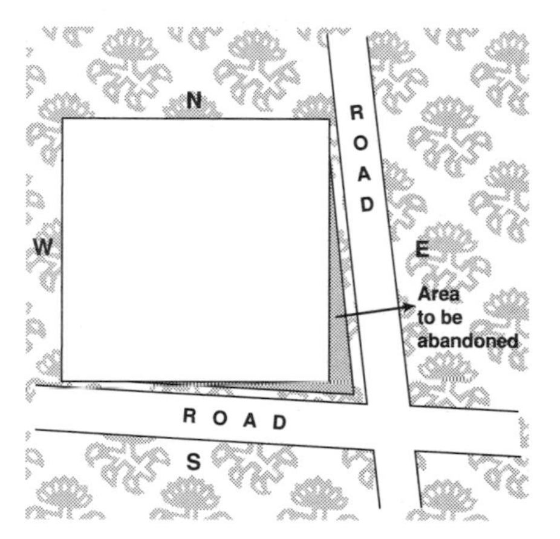

Fig. 69: Southeast extension

Figure 70: The Southwest is extended, both in the Southern Southwest and the Western Southwest, and can be corrected by the abandonment of the marked area.

Figure 71: The Northwest extension in both the Northern Northwest and the Western Northwest is corrected by the abandonment of the marked area.

Figure 72: A Southern Southeast extension can be corrected by creating a cut in the Southern Southwest, which is suitable, and abandoning the shaded area.

Figure 73: A Southern Southwest extension can be corrected by creating a cut in the Southern Southeast, which is suitable, and abandoning the shaded area.

Figure 74: An extension in the Western Northwest can be corrected as shown, creating a Western Southwest cut, which is suitable, and abandoning the shaded area.

Figure 75: If the Western Southwest is extended, it can be corrected as shown, creating a cut in the Western Northwest, which is suitable, and abandoning the shaded area.

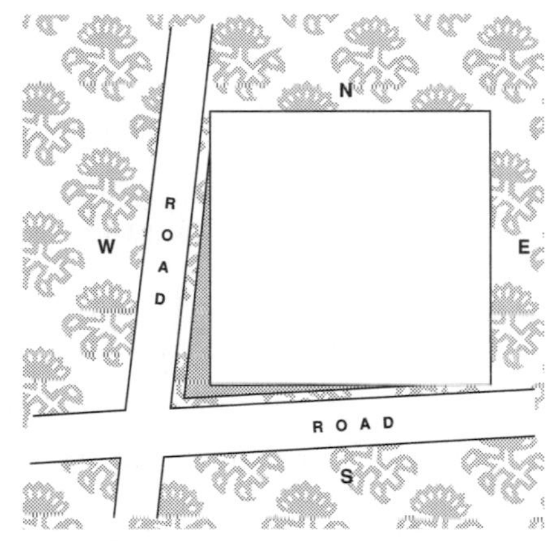

Fig. 70: Southwest extension

Fig. 71: Northwest extension

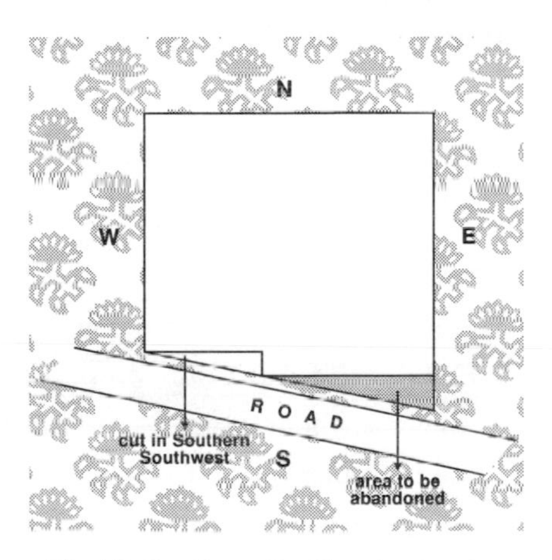

Fig. 72: Southern Southeast extension

Fig. 73: Southern Southwest extension

Fig. 74: Western Northwest extension

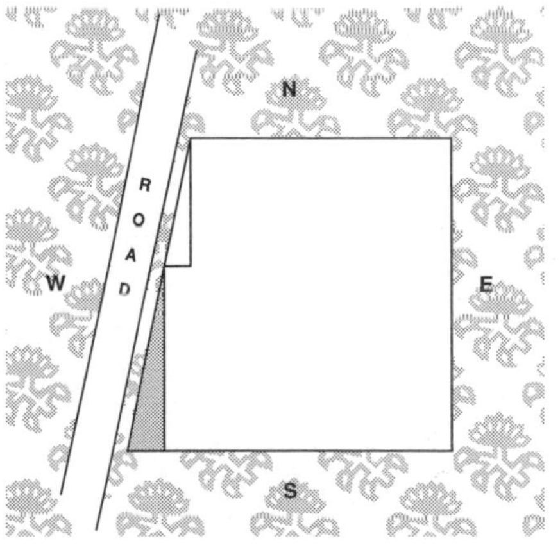

Fig. 75: Western Southwest extension

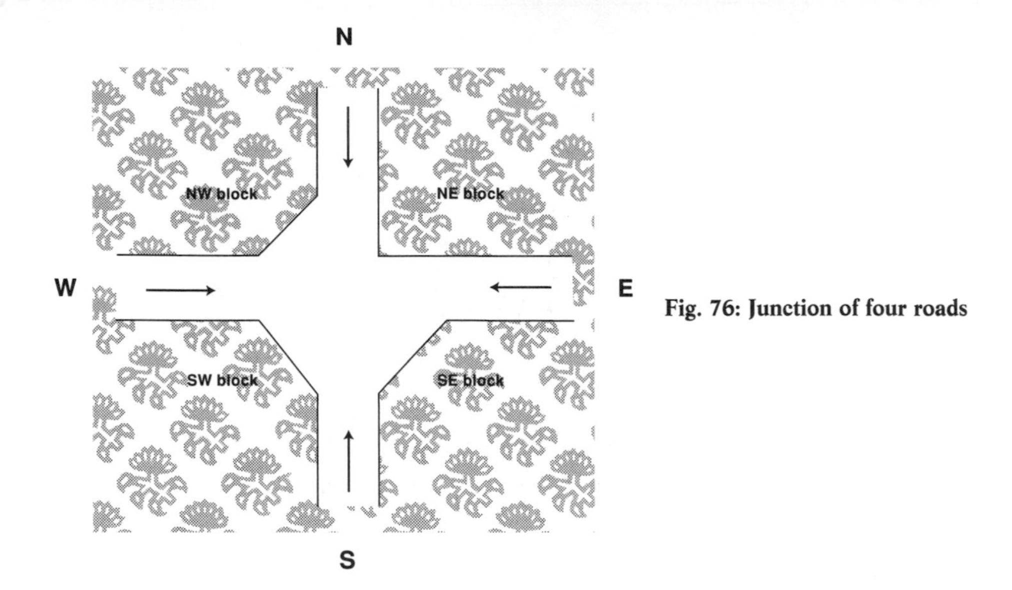

Fig. 76: Junction of four roads

A particular situation regarding cuts is created by the junction of four roads (fig. 76). Whenever four roads meet, the Northeast block should not be truncated. If it is truncated, any business or house situated there will experience negative effects of vaastu because a Northeast cut is not acceptable.

DIFFERENT SHAPES OF PLOTS

Lots with irregular shapes, and those in the shape of circles, ovals, and triangles are generally not considered good vaastu. However, in the case of very large properties, the general topography is more important than the exact boundaries. Also, triangular plots with Northeastern extension—as shown in figures 77 and 78—are considered to be suitable.

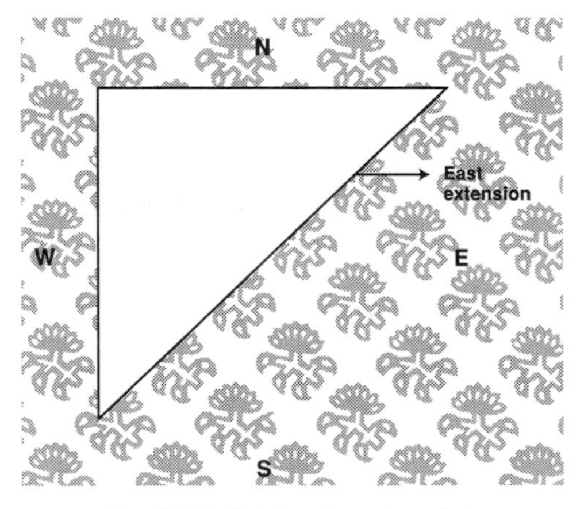

Fig. 77: Suitable triangular plot

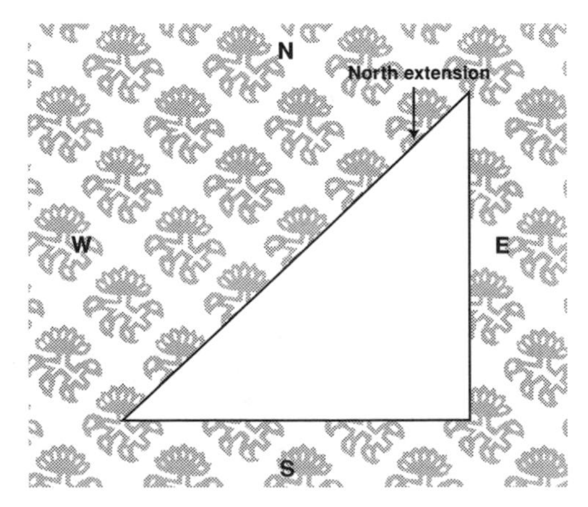

Fig. 78: Suitable triangular plot

CHAPTER 12

STREET FOCUS
(VEEDI SHOLA)

ANOTHER FACTOR OF SERIOUS CONSIDERATION in vaastu is the location of street focus in relation to a plot of land. Street focus—created by the intersection of a street with a piece of property—has the effect of intensifying the influence of the side it focuses on. If the focus is to an exalted side it will bring bountiful good results, while if it is to a debilitated position, severe unwanted consequences may result. Figure 79 shows the eight different possible types of street focus and their impact.

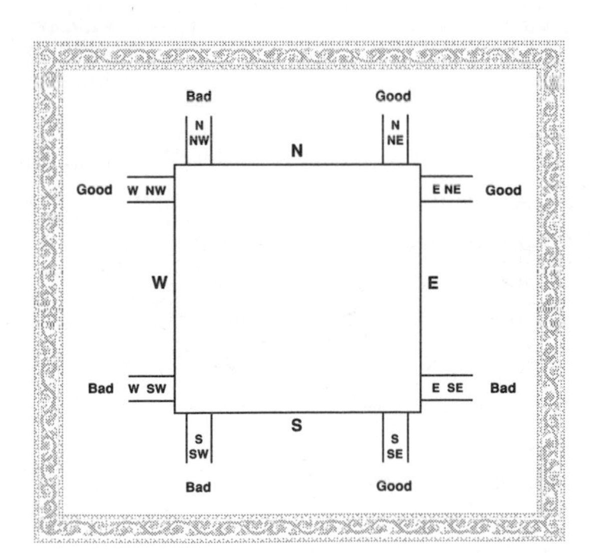

Fig. 79: Street Focus

In a few cases a bad street focus can be corrected. For example, a street focus to a debilitated position can be corrected by constructing a wall on the side of the property where the focus occurs, as high as the tallest part of the building there. If future construction takes place, the height of the wall must also be raised to match the new height of the building.

Alternatively, a small shop or a shed can be built at the street focus and then sold. Figure 80 shows how to correct a street focus in the Eastern Southeast by cutting off a portion of the Southeast corner, building a shop or shed on it, and then selling it. The shop gets a very good vaastu by having a road focus in the Eastern Northeast, which will make the business flourish.

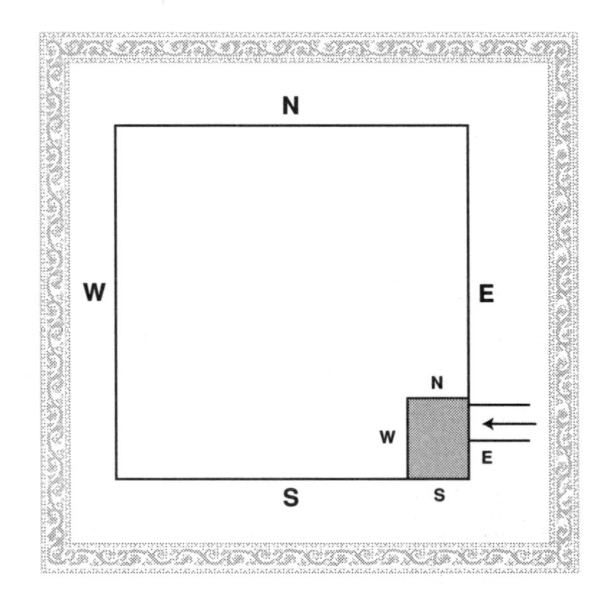

Fig. 80: Street focus to Eastern Southeast and its correction

The impact of street focus on the well-being of the home's inhabitants is very powerful. Soon after his graduation a friend of mine built a small software company. After a year he moved into a new house with a street focus in the Eastern Northeast, which is very positive. Within six months his company was bought out for one hundred million (U.S.) dollars, and within the next year his stock options in the new company were worth over three hundred million dollars.

Alternatively, a relative of mine moved into a new rented house with a Northern Northwest street focus. When my vaastu teacher, Geretta Reddy, came to know of it, he asked my relative to move out of the house immediately because the Northern Northwest focus was putting his young child's life at risk.

The street focus clearly enhances the vaastu effect immensely, either to a positive or negative side. In feng shui, a road focus is considered inauspicious. However, vaastu takes a different view when the street focus is on an exalted position.

CHAPTER 13

PROJECTION

THE PROJECTION OF A BUILDING into a street creates a street focus. For example, if a building facing East or North projects into the street, it gets a street focus from the North or East—a good feature. When a building projects into the street in the South or the West, the street focus is on a debilitated position—with bad results.

Figure 81 shows a projection into a street on the North side, which produces road focus on the Western Northwest and Eastern Northeast, both exalted positions. This brings very good results, especially for a business.

Figure 82 shows a projection into an Eastern street, which produces road focus on the Northern Northeast and Southern Southeast, both exalted positions. This brings good results, especially for a business.

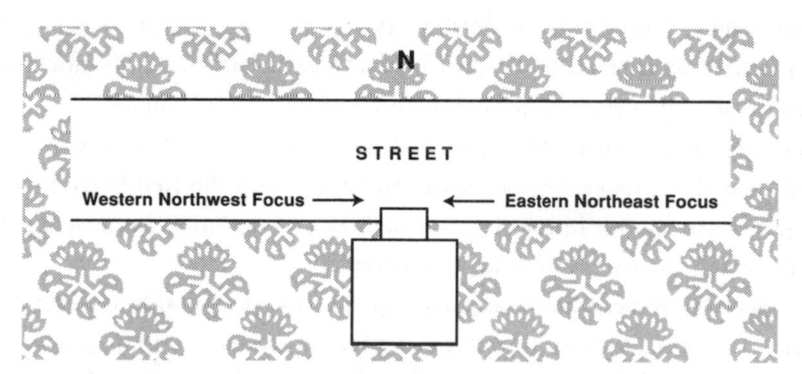

Fig. 81: Effect of projection into street on North side

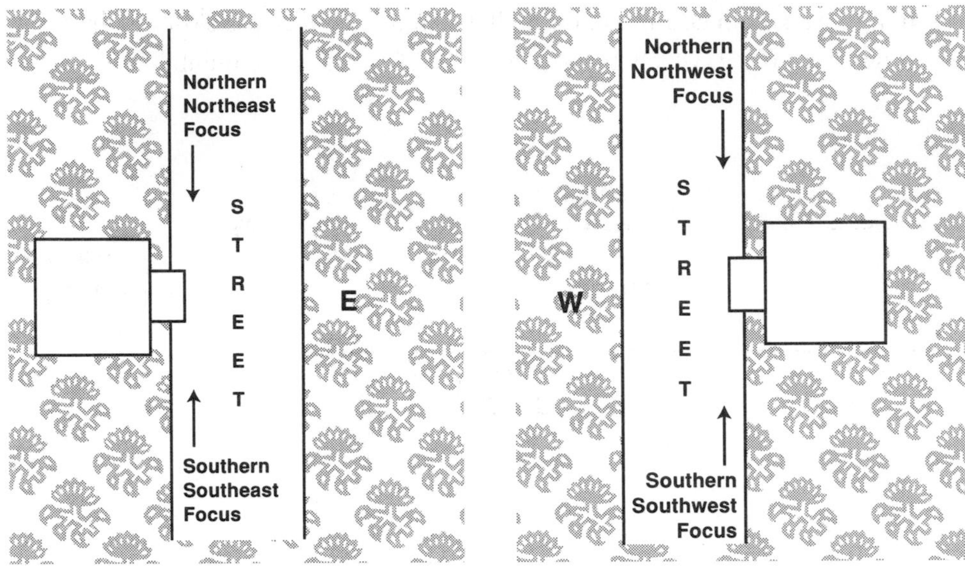

Fig. 82: Effect of projection into street on East side

Fig. 84: Effect of projection into street on West side

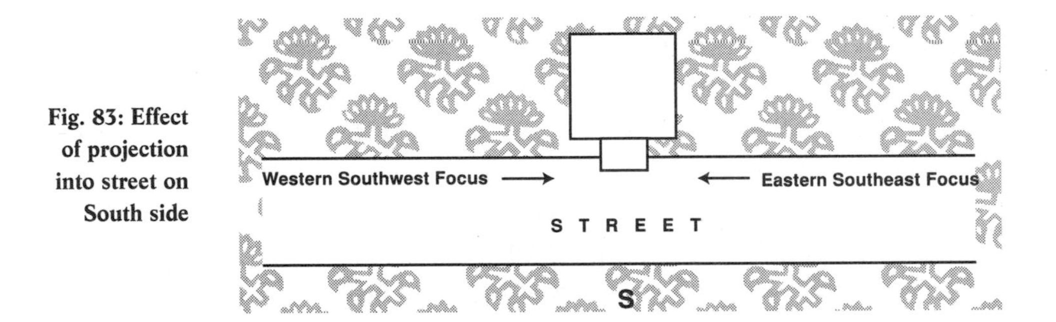

Fig. 83: Effect of projection into street on South side

A projection into a street to the South (fig. 83) produces road focus on the Eastern Southeast and the Western Southwest, both of which are debilitated positions, causing losses in business.

A projection into a street to the West (fig. 84) produces road focus on the Southern Southwest and Northern Northwest, both of which are debilitated positions, causing losses in business.

The projection of neighboring houses also influences the vaastu of one's house. If your home is in a row of houses, the houses to the East or North should not project farther to the East or North than your house. If, however, the houses to the West or South project farther, that is a good situation. In figure 85, house number 2 is closer to the street than house number 1. This will create a negative effect on house number 1 because it blocks the positive Northeast energy.

In figure 86, both houses are facing East. House number 1 is closer to the street than house number 2, which brings a negative effect to house number 2.

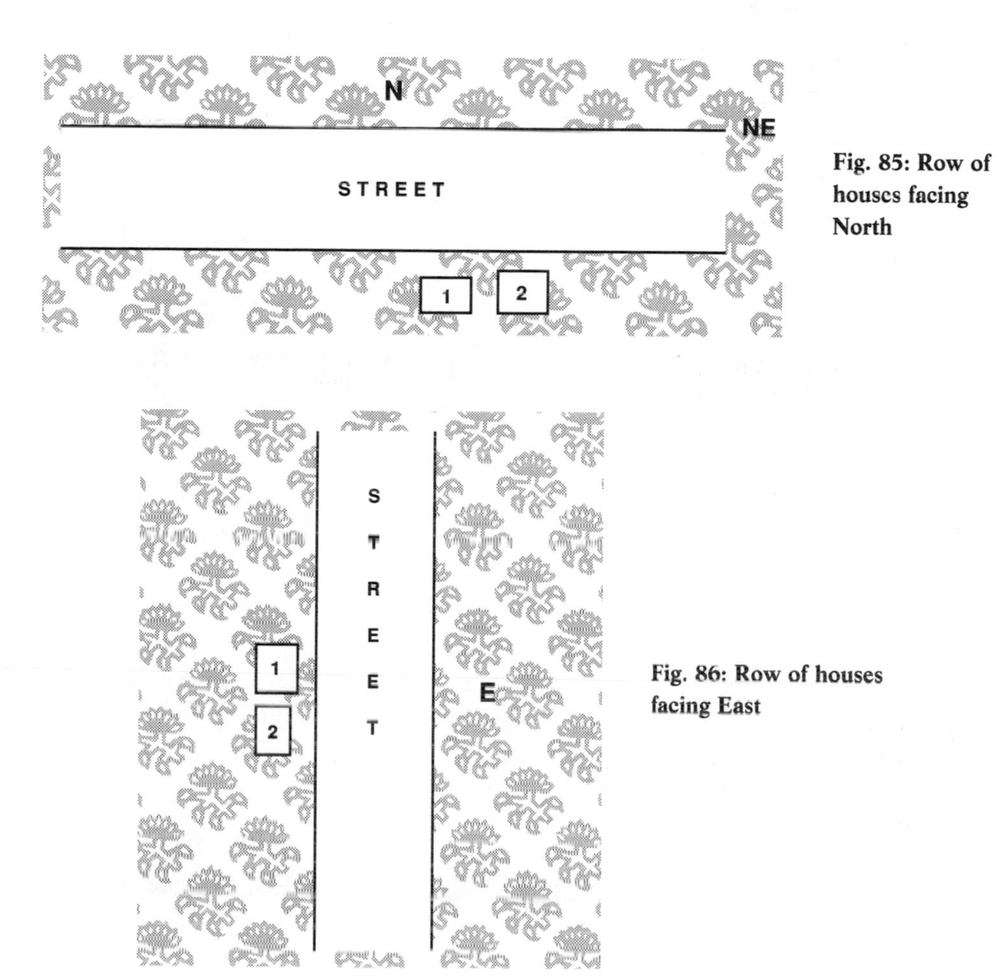

Fig. 85: Row of houses facing North

Fig. 86: Row of houses facing East

CHAPTER 14

CLOSURE OF CORNERS AND RECTIFICATION

THE VAASTU EFFECTS OF A PIECE OF PROPERTY are changed whenever there is a closure of a corner such as that created by a wall or fence. There are several things one can do to correct this problem. For example, if there is a closure at the Southwest corner (fig. 87) it is a good feature. But there should not be any well or slope down toward the West or South of the structure. If these conditions are present, a gap of 2 to 3 feet should be left between the building and the compound wall or fence.

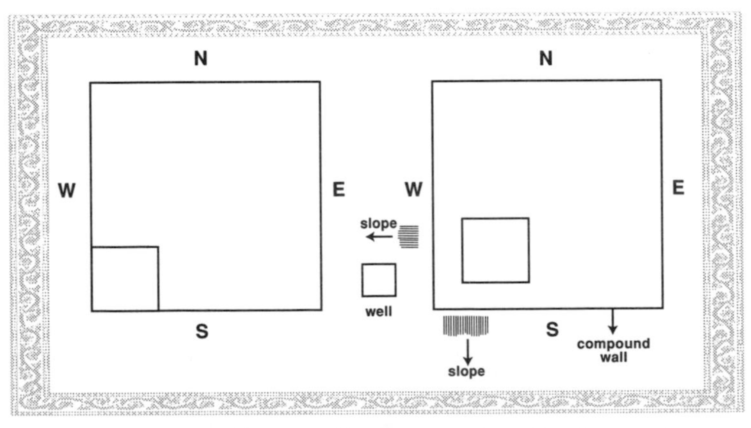

Fig. 87: Closure of Southwest and rectification

A closure to the Northwest, shown in figure 88, causes unwarranted mental tension. It can be rectified by having open space toward the North and the West. At minimum, a gap of 2 to 3 feet should be left between the building and the compound wall or fence.

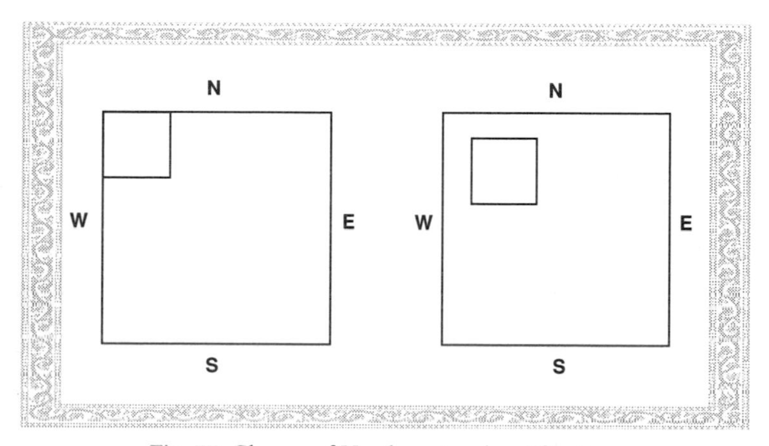

Fig. 88: Closure of Northwest and rectification

Closure to the Northeast (fig. 89) causes loss of progeny and general diminution in progress and prosperity. If there is open space toward the North and the East, the defect is somewhat rectified. However, the Northeast should not be heavier or higher than the other three corners—the Southeast, Northwest, and Southwest.

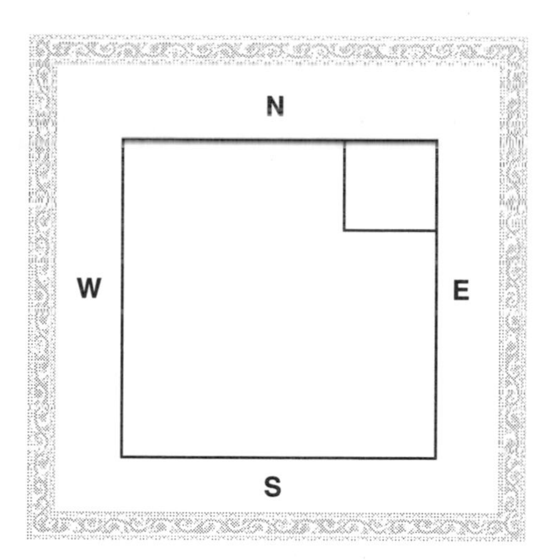

Fig. 89: Closure of Northeast

A family I had helped financially bought a plot in which the Northeast was closed with a small building that could not be removed because of various difficulties. The owner put a gate in the Western Northwest and built a small house on the

Southwest side. These measures created beneficial effects: he became well known in his business and soon prospered. But he could not rectify the Northeast closure and was always short of funds. After a year of growth and struggle he was forced to leave that place.

A closure of the Southeast, as shown in figure 90, causes problems such as disagreements among family members. It mostly affects the female children, especially the second child. Creating open space in the East and the South rectifies the defect. If there is no open space, a gap of 2 to 3 feet should be left between the building and the compound wall.

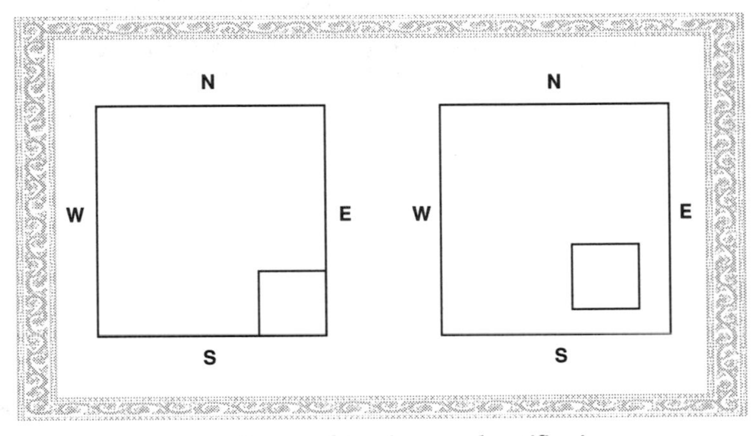

Fig. 90: Closure of Southeast and rectification

CHAPTER 15

WELLS, SEPTIC TANKS, AND WATER BODIES

VAASTU IS SIGNIFICANTLY INFLUENCED by the position or direction of wells, septic tanks, and water bodies such as ponds or lakes. It is also influenced by the direction the water is flowing in nearby channels such as rivers, streams, and drainage. Overhead water storage tanks and the storage of chemicals also play a significant role in vaastu. Figure 91 indicates the recommended directions.

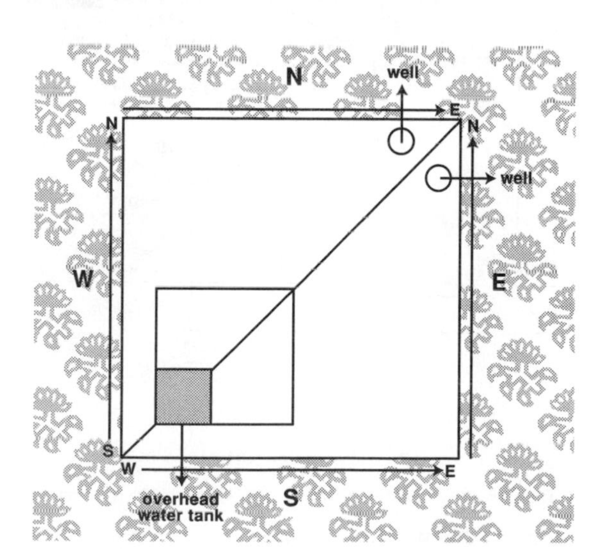

Fig. 91: Direction of water flow and location of wells

The direction of flow of drainage, rivers, and streams should be from South to North and from West to East. If a waterfall is included in the landscaping around the home, it should be placed on the Southeast side with the stream flowing toward North. However, the flow of a river from East to West on the North side has a special significance. It has been observed that the purity and potency of medicinal plants are enhanced when fed by water that flows in a westward direction *(paschimavaahini).* This phenomenon is explained by the influence of the planets associated with the West and the East. Saturn governs dirt and impurities in the West and the Sun brings purity in the East. A river flowing to the West thus carries the Sun's purifying energy to the plants.

Open wells and drilled or bore wells should be located either to the Northern Northeast or to the Eastern Northeast (fig. 92). They should not be on the line joining the Northeast corner of the house with the Northeast corner of the plot or on the line joining the Northeast and the Southwest corners of the plot. Septic tanks should be either at center North or center East (fig. 92). The storage of chemicals and petroleum should be in the central North or central East.

Some ancient texts of vaastu recommend the central West as a good place for a well. This is because Varuna, the god of water, also governs the Western direction. But having a well at the West reduces its weight and height, making it lower than the East, with negative effects. Hence, modern vaastu experts do not think it is correct to have a well in the West.

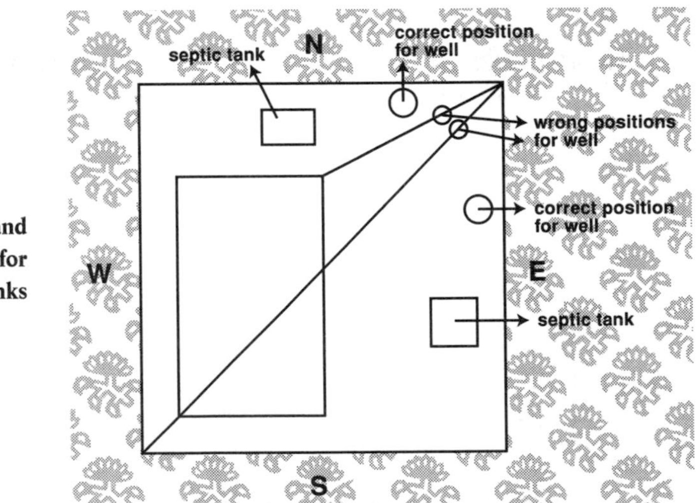

Fig. 92: Correct and incorrect locations for wells and septic tanks

Another important consideration regarding the location of a well or underground storage tank is its relationship to a gate or door. As shown in figure 93, if the gate is in the Northern Northeast, the well should be to the West side of the gate. If the gate is in the Eastern Northeast, the well should be to the South side of the gate.

An overhead tank should be placed in the Southwest corner since it increases the height and weight (fig. 94). Some books recommend leaving 2 to 3 feet of space around an overhead tank. Others recommend that a tank be located on the Western Southwest side next to the diagonal line joining the Southwest and Northeast. However, my teacher strongly recommends that an overhead water tank be placed at the Southwest corner without leaving space around it. If the overhead tank is not on top of the roof, it can be built outside toward the Southwest corner. If it touches the house, it should be the tallest structure. One should be careful not to create a Southwest extension.

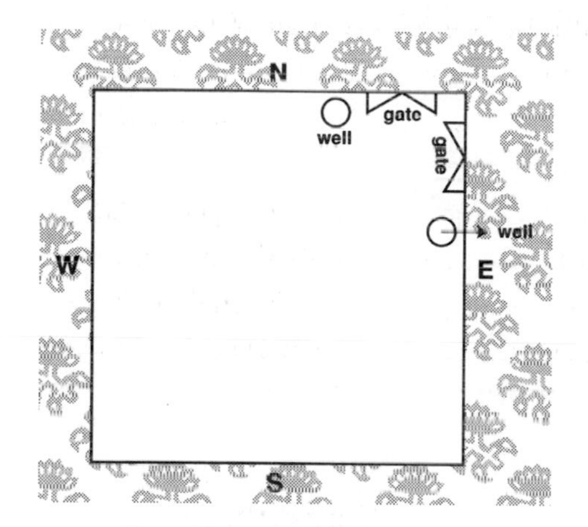

Fig. 93: Location of front gate and well

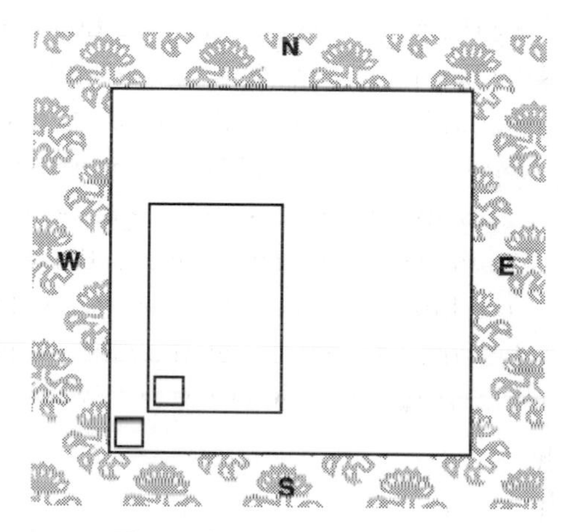

Fig. 94: Water tank locations

PART FOUR

CONSTRUCTION PRINCIPLES

CHAPTER 16

POSITIONING A HOUSE ON A PLOT

TO DETERMINE WHERE TO POSITION a house on a piece of property, the precepts of vaastu indicate that there should be more space in the North than in the South and more space in the East than in the West, as shown in figure 95. In other words, the house should be positioned more toward the Southwest side of the property.

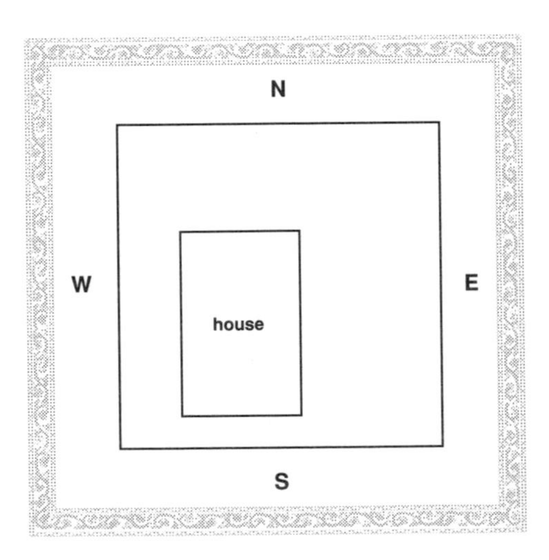

Fig. 95: Positioning a house on a plot

If the plot is on an angle, the house should be positioned as shown in figure 96. The house position need not be rotated, but it should be constructed in such a way that the foundation perimeters are parallel to the property lines with more space in the North than in the South and more space in the East than in the West.

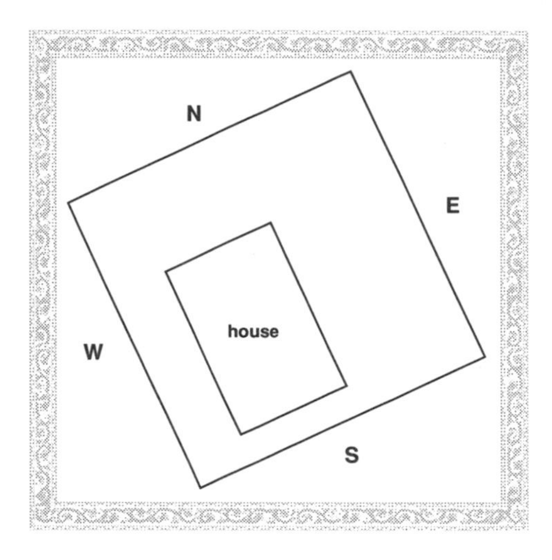

Fig. 96: Plot rotated 25 degrees toward the Northwest

While positioning the house in a diagonal plot, equal space should be kept on all sides (fig. 97).

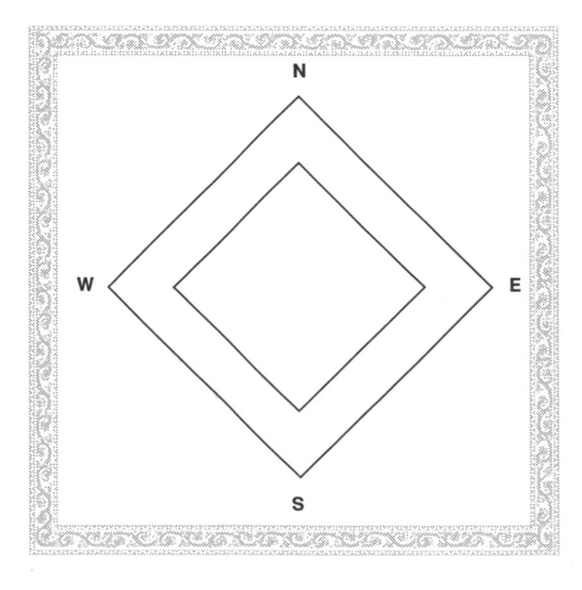

Fig. 97: Diagonal plot and house position

CHAPTER 17

GROUNDBREAKING (*BHUMI POOJA*)

THE ANCIENT VAASTU TEXTS CONTAIN elaborate descriptions of the rituals to be performed at the groundbreaking (and housewarming) of a home, as well as detailed methods of determining the most auspicious date and time for the ceremonies. The intent of the groundbreaking ceremony is to pray for divine blessings before construction begins. Although the Indian rituals do not easily translate into Western settings, the same intent can be observed by those of any faith, using their own traditional ways of asking for blessings. In any case, one's sincerity and faith are the key to auspicious results.

In Indian communities, a proper day and time *(Muhoorta)* for the groundbreaking or *Bhumi Pooja* is determined by a learned vedic astrologer. Based on the owner's natal chart and birth stars, an auspicious moment is determined. For those who do not have the services of an astrologer, the owner's birth date can be used. A learned priest is invited that day and proper offerings are made to different deities, including Vaastupurusha and Ganesha, who removes all obstacles. A request is made to the gods for permission to build a dwelling and for blessings on the construction. After this ritual, the ground is first broken by the owner and then by the architect *(sthapati)* or the chief mason *(vardhaki)*. *Bhoomi Pooja* should not be done during the period when any female members of the family are pregnant, as

this is known to cause miscarriages or birth defects. The groundbreaking should be done in the Northeast sector, toward the center of the plot. It should not be done in the Northeast corner or on the diagonal of the plot. (See figure 98.)

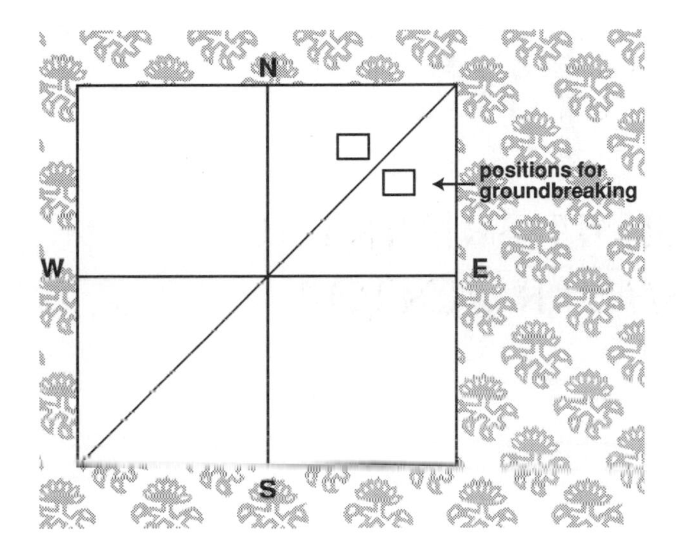

Fig. 98: Positions for groundbreaking

CHAPTER 18

BEGINNING CONSTRUCTION

AFTER THE GROUNDBREAKING, construction begins with digging for the foundation (fig. 99), which should start from the Northeast corner and proceed toward the Northwest corner and then from the Northeast to the Southeast corner. Then it should proceed from the Northwest to the Southwest and the Southeast to the Southwest. This conforms to the height and weight principle as the reduction in weight proceeds from Northeast to Northwest, Northeast to Southeast, Northwest to Southwest, and finally Southeast to Southwest.

Since the laying of the foundation adds weight, it should follow the reverse order (fig. 100), proceeding from the Southwest to the Southeast, then from the Southwest to the Northwest, then from the Southeast to the Northeast, and finally from the Northwest to the Northeast.

Also using the height and weight principle, the direction of construction should proceed from the Southwest sector to the Southeast sector, then toward the Northwest sector and finally toward the Northeast sector.

During construction, all construction material should be stored or placed on the South and the West sides, keeping the North and the East free. If large amounts of materials have to be stored and there is a shortage of space, the North and the East sides may be used, as long as heavier materials are stored on the South and the West sides. Under no circumstances should the Northeast be blocked.

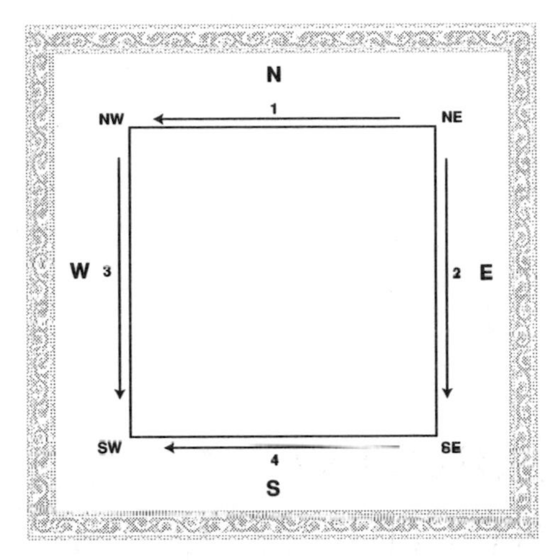

Fig. 99: Digging for foundation

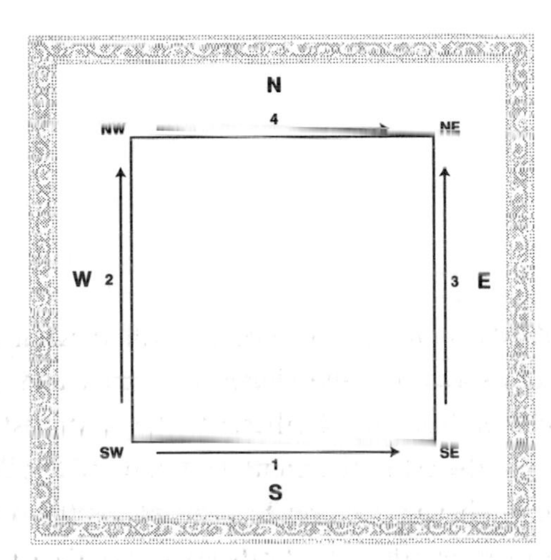

Fig. 100: Laying foundation

CHAPTER 19

CONVERGENT AND DIVERGENT STRUCTURES

U-SHAPED BUILDINGS WITH three sides are called convergent structures and L-shaped buildings with two sides are called divergent structures. An opening to the North or the East is considered good vaastu (figs. 101–2) and an opening to the West or the South is not (figs. 103–4).

In a divergent structure, an opening to the Southeast can bring misfortune (fig. 105) while an opening to the Southwest can cause the premature death of the

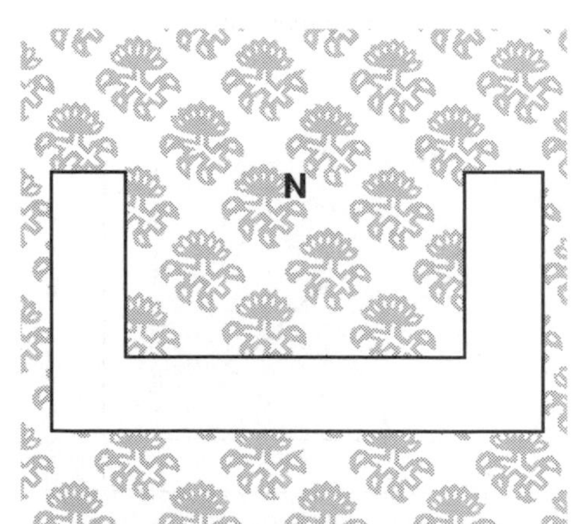

Fig. 101: North convergent structure—positive effects

Fig. 102: East convergent structure—positive effects

Fig. 103: West convergent structure—negative effects

Fig. 104: South convergent structure—negative effects

inhabitants (fig. 106). If the Northeast is open, it brings beneficial results (fig. 107), while if the Northwest is open, it can bring many kinds of negative results (fig. 108).

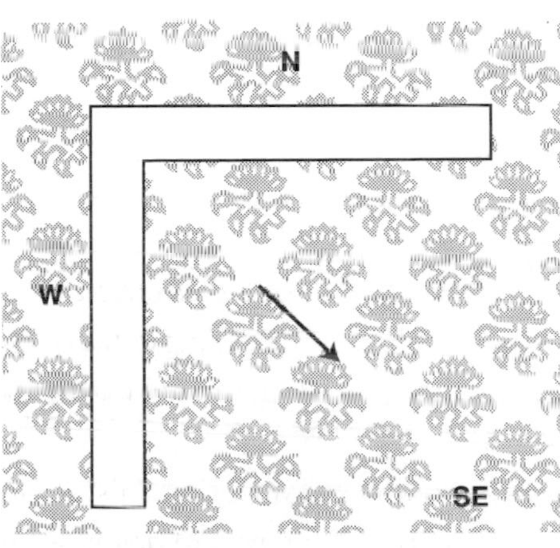

Fig. 105: Southeast divergent structure—negative effects

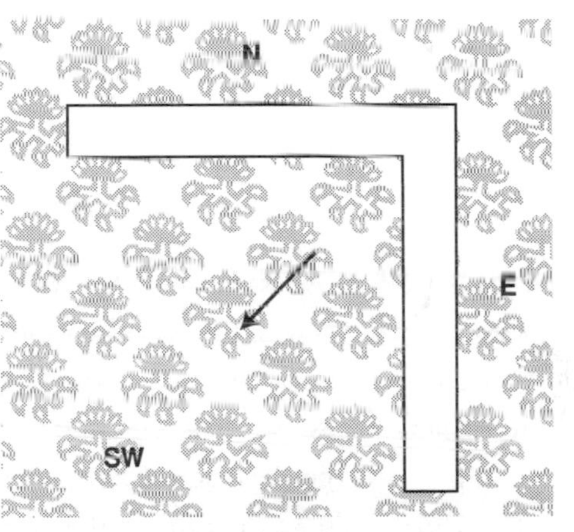

Fig. 106: Southwest divergent structure—negative effects

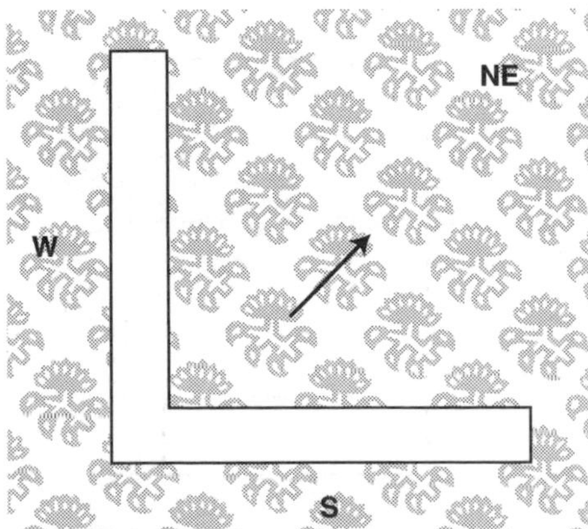

Fig. 107: Northeast divergent structure—positive effects

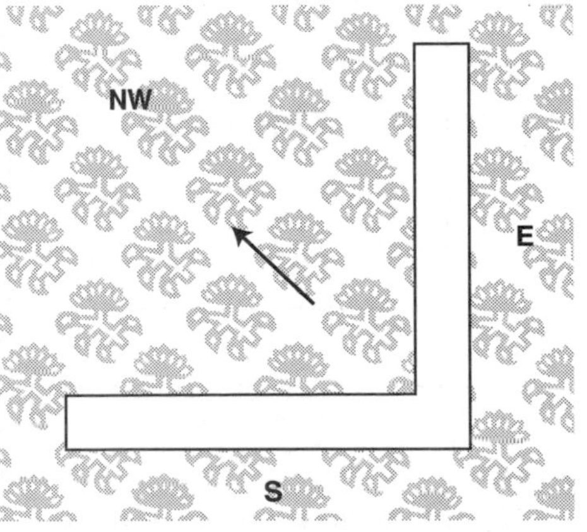

Fig. 108: Northwest divergent structure—negative effects

CHAPTER 20

MULTIPLE BUILDINGS WITHIN A COMPOUND

WHENEVER THERE IS MORE THAN ONE independent building within a compound, each building should have more space toward North than toward South and more space toward East than toward West. Figure 109 shows the proper placement of multiple buildings within a compound wall or fence.

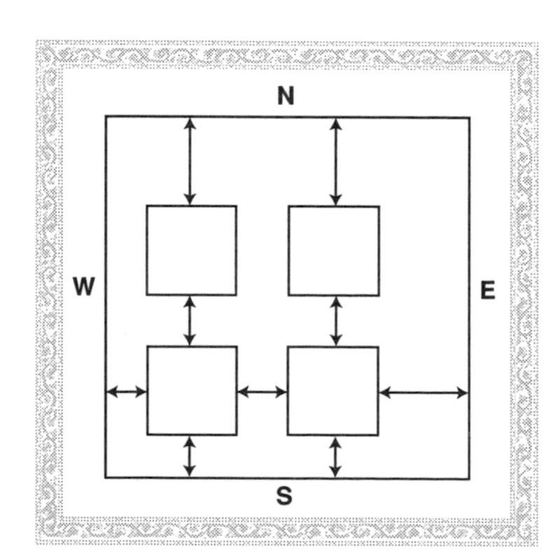

Fig. 109: Placement of multiple buildings within a compound wall or fence

GUEST HOUSES AND GUEST ROOMS

The Northwest part of a plot is good for a guest house, since guests come to enjoy and do not stay for a long time. It is also best to locate a guest room in the Northwest sector of the house.

DOMESTICATED ANIMALS

Housing for cows, dogs, and other pets should be to the Northwest side of a dwelling because Vaayu, the deity of the Northwest, governs animals.

RENTING OUT PART OF THE PROPERTY

If a building or part of a building that is in the Northeast sector of a plot is rented out and the owner lives in any of the other three sectors, all the benefits of the Northeast sector will be enjoyed by the renters. Because of this, only structures in the Southwest, Northwest, and Southeast sectors should be rented. The owner should live in the Northeast sector if any other area is rented. If no other area is rented, the owner must live in the Southwest sector and keep the Northeast sector of the building or plot vacant.

CHAPTER 21

LOCATING ROOMS AND FUNCTIONAL SYSTEMS

FIGURE 110 SHOWS A SAMPLE house plan with optimum locations for different rooms.

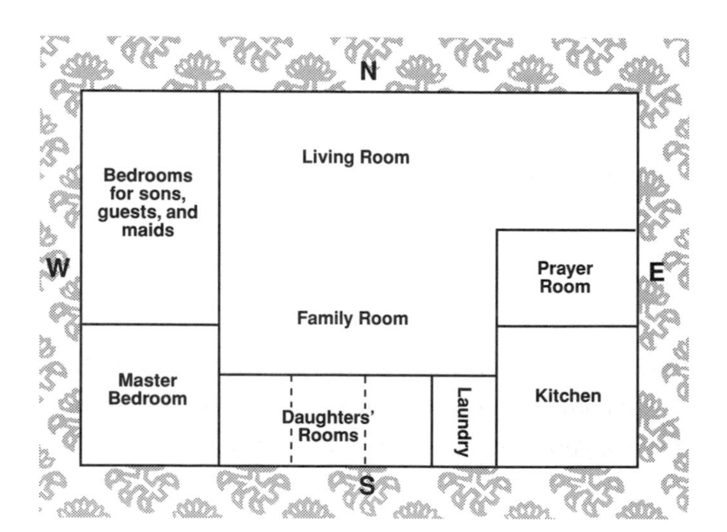

Fig. 110: Room locations for different functions

PRAYER ROOM

Prayer or *pooja* rooms are traditionally located in the Northeast sector of the house. However, according to vaastu, a prayer room could also be in the Southeast or the Northwest sector. The deity should face the East or the North and the altar should be against the West or the South wall. The central part of the house, governed by the element ether and called *Brahmasthana,* is a particularly auspicious place for the deity and prayer room. In figure 111, four positions for prayer rooms are shown with possible door and altar positions.

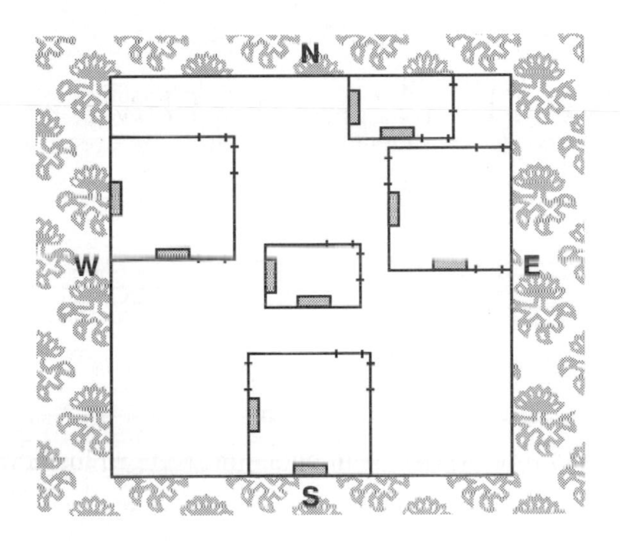

Fig. 111: Different locations for prayer room

Since prayer rooms are small, the entire wall could be a door with or without windows. If there are windows, they should be on both sides. Windows on the sides of a door are considered as representing the eyes of a person. When there is only one window attached to a door frame, it brings eye problems to the inhabitants. In some unfortunate situations even severe injury and blindness may occur.

OFFICE OR LIBRARY

Because of the influence of the governing planets Jupiter and Ketu, and the deity Ishana, knowledge and wisdom come from the Northeast. Thus, the Northeast sector is a good location for an office or library.

KITCHEN

The best location for the kitchen is the Southeast sector of the dwelling. The second best area for the kitchen is the Northwest side. If it is not possible to have the kitchen in the Southeast or the Northwest, the third best area is the Southwest. Wherever the kitchen is, the cooking range should be placed in the Southeast corner of the kitchen, situated so that the person cooking will be facing the East. There should be a gap of 2 to 3 inches between the wall and the range.

The kitchen should never be in the Northeast corner of the house, since this brings suffering to male progeny, such as health problems and financial difficulties. In my experience this has proved consistently true. Although in some parts of South India, especially in Kerala State, some vaastu traditions recommend placing kitchens in the Northeast, modern vaastu experts think that this is not appropriate.

TREASURY

A treasury or money and jewel storage safe should be on the North side because the North is governed by the god of wealth, Kubera. However, it should not touch the North wall; a few inches of space should be left between them.

BEDROOMS

The master bedroom should be in the Southwest sector. The Southwest corner is governed by Rahu and Niruti, both of which have a malefic influence. However, if the master of the house occupies this region the malefic influence is transformed into a beneficial influence. In countries such as India where it is common to have overhead water storage tanks, the furniture in the room underneath the tank should be arranged so that the bed is not under the tank. Preferably, a closet can be built under it.

A daughter's bedroom should be to the Southeast side of the master bedroom since the South governs and is auspicious for the female members of the family, fostering good performance in school, wholesome marital relationships, and all around prosperity. A son's bedroom should be to the Northwest side of the master bedroom since the West governs and is auspicious for the male members of the family. Bedrooms in the East cause ill health to the occupants and bedrooms in the North result in financial losses, while bedrooms in the West result in a peaceful and prosperous life and bedrooms in the South ensure good health.

GUEST ROOM AND SERVANTS' QUARTERS

A guest room or a room for the use of a maid or servant should be in the Northwest corner. The Northwest is governed by the Moon and *vaayu* (air element), representing movement, and guests stay only for short periods. Placing the room of a maid or servant in this corner will foster their appropriate behavior and good relationship with the owner.

TOILETS AND BATHROOMS

Toilets and bathrooms should not be in the Northeast corner or in the center of the house, and should be placed either to the East or North side of a bedroom. They should not be on the West or South sides unless there is an adjoining bedroom to the West or South and the bathroom is common to both rooms. In figure 112, bedrooms 1 and 3 have bathrooms to their South and West. This would not otherwise be correct but is so in this case, because bedroom 2 is to the South of bedroom 1 and to the West of bedroom 3.

If the toilet is a standard Western commode, it can be placed in the Southwest corner of the bathroom. If it is the Asian squatting type, it should not be in the Southwest corner as it lowers the Southwest.

Fig. 112: Toilet and bathroom locations

CELLARS AND BASEMENTS

A basement or cellar underneath the entire house is acceptable. If the cellar or basement is built under only part of the house, the preferred location is under the Northeast side because that makes the Northeast lower, a good vaastu feature. If more basement area is required, it should be added first under the Northwest sector of the house and then under the Southeast sector, resulting in a basement under all sectors except the Southwest. A basement placed under the Southwest sector of the house brings untoward effects such as ill health, financial losses, and mental depression, unless all sectors under the house are included.

Because of the lack of sunshine, bedrooms in basements are not advisable.

GRANARY

The storage of farm produce or inventory should be in the Northwest. In a factory, if the inventory moves out through the Western Northwest door or gate, the business will flourish.

STAIRCASE

If the building requires a staircase, it should be located on the Northwest or the Southeast side (fig. 113), and never on the Northeast side or in the center *(Brahmasthana).* A Northeast staircase causes severe financial losses and heart problems. If the staircase is circular, it should turn in a clockwise direction. There should not be a room under a staircase. The starting direction of the staircase should be toward the South or the West and any landing should face either the North or the East. An odd number of steps is better since if one starts with the right foot, one will also land with the right foot.

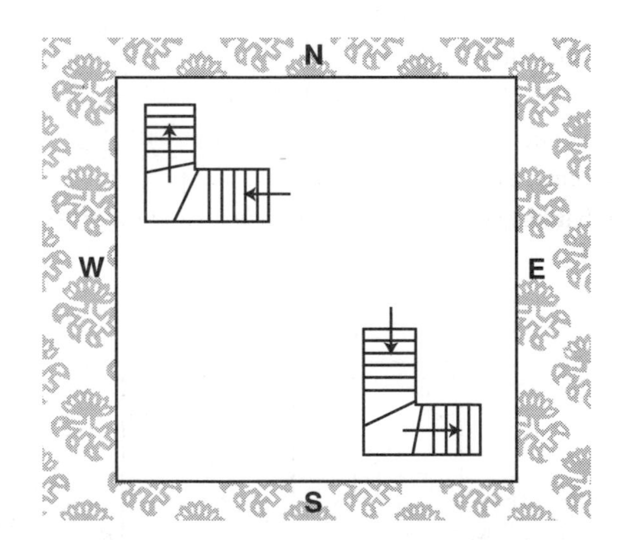

Fig. 113: Locations for staircases

MECHANICAL FUNCTIONS

The Southeast is governed by the deity of fire, Agni. Thus, all mechanical functions such as furnaces, water heaters, boilers, and electrical panels should be located in the Southeast sector.

CHAPTER 22

PLACEMENT OF DOORS, GATES, AND WINDOWS

THE RECOMMENDED POSITIONS for doors and gates are based on the exalted and debilitated positions (fig. 114). The traditional vaastu system has several different methodologies of placing main doors and gates, which sometimes conflict with each other. The modern system of vaastu proposes the following consistent approach, one that has been found to be beneficial and more applicable to the modern lifestyle.

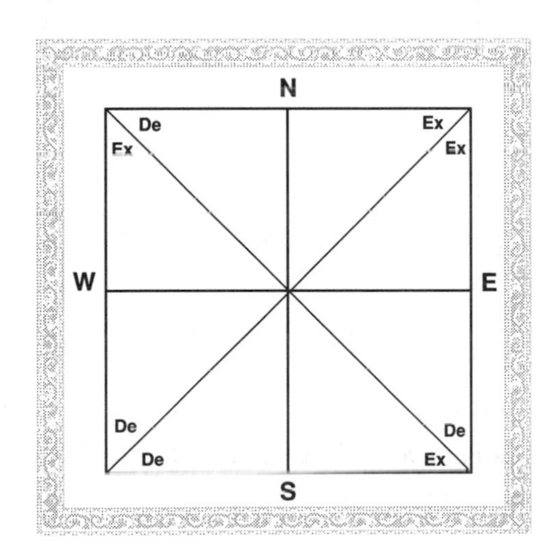

Fig. 114: Exalted and debilitated positions

There are several basic rules one should follow. The primary rule is that doors and gates should be placed in exalted positions. Movement from one door to another should go from exalted to exalted positions, as shown in figure 115, not from debilitated to debilitated positions (fig. 116).

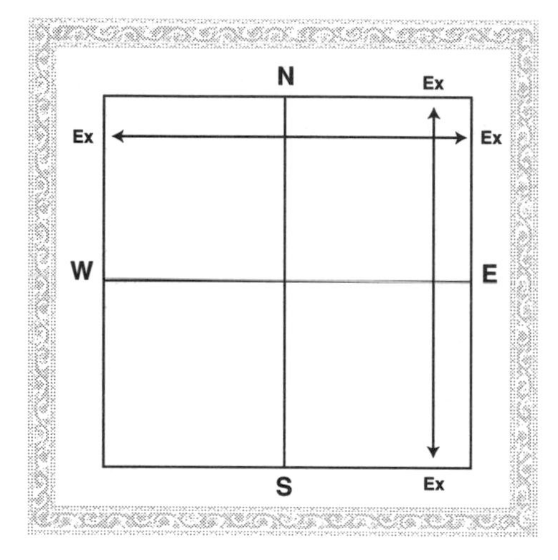

Fig 115: Movement from exalted to exalted positions

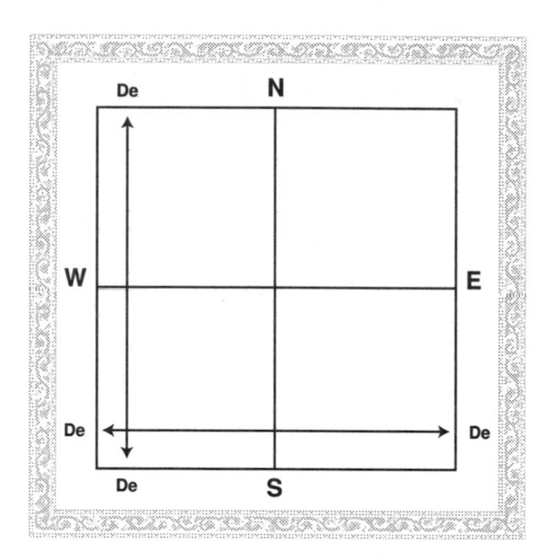

Fig 116: Movement from debilitated to debilitated positions

COMPOUND WALLS OR FENCES

If compound walls or fences are built, they should be of equal height on all four sides or higher in the West and the South and lower in the East and the North. The Southwest corner must be set to 90 degrees and should not have any rounding. The Northwest and Southeast corners must be 90 degrees or more, and the Northeast corner should be 90 degrees or less. Compound walls should not be broken or left in a dilapidated condition, especially in debilitated positions, as this attracts bad luck. It is said that the malefic forces get concentrated in these areas. Whenever there is a house toward the North or the East, a compound wall or fence is necessary. Otherwise the wall of the neighboring house acts as a compound wall or fence that will be higher and bring bad results.

EXTERIOR DOORS

The front and back doors of a house should be placed so that there is less space on the wall to the outside than on the inside, as shown in figure 117. Placing them in the center of the wall is also acceptable.

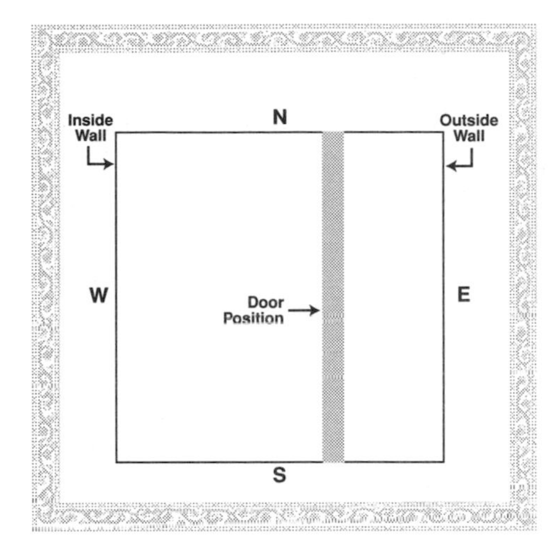

Fig. 117: The correct position of a door on a wall.

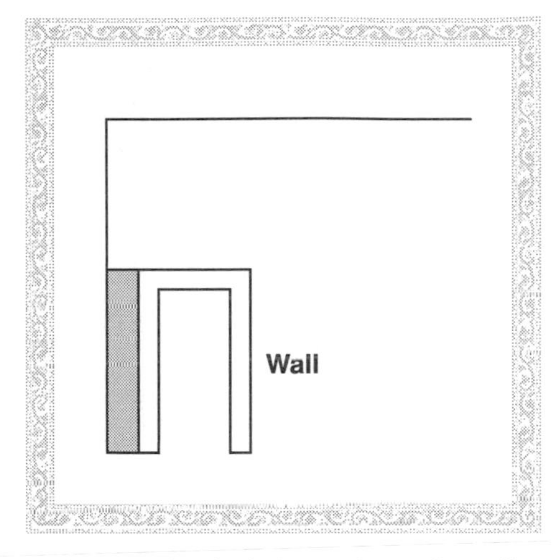

Fig. 118: The shaded area shows the wall space between the door and the main wall.

A door should not be fixed contiguous to the main wall of the house (fig. 118). A minimum of 4 inches of wall should be left before fixing the door frame to a lateral wall.

Although there may be other exalted positions, it is preferable to fix the front door in the exalted position facing the road.

The front door of the house should be wider than the back door. If there is a door in line with and facing the front door, it should not be wider than the front door. The front and back doors should have thresholds. Other doors may or may not have them.

NUMBERS OF OPENINGS IN A WALL

Vaastu considers all odd numbers except the number one to be inauspicious since they create an imbalance in the energy flow. To balance the flow of energy, there must be an even number of items such as doors, windows, or columns. Thus, there should not be three doors to a wall (fig. 119) or three gates to a compound wall on any side.

An odd number of doors, windows, or columns constitutes a defect in the body of Vaastupurusha, the subtle essence of the body of everyone in the house. When there is a defect in Vaastupurusha's body, it will start manifesting in family members, even though it could take more than one generation for the defect to manifest. This kind of defect is known to bring injury to the inhabitants' bodily organs such as eyes, ears, and limbs. One vaastu book gives a tragic reference to this testimony. For more than two generations, all the children of a family that lived in a house with three doors to a wall were born blind. However, there will be no vaastu defect if three doors are in a line in different walls.

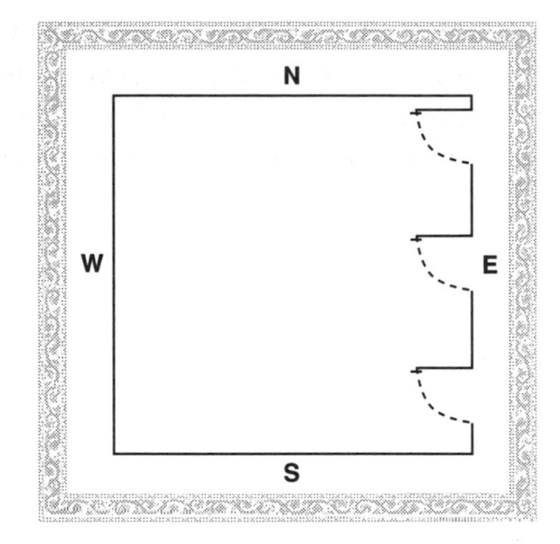

Fig. 119: Three doors in the same wall—not acceptable

CORRECTION OF DEFECTS INVOLVING DOORS AND GATES

In the case of a house facing East with a gate placed in front of the main door, another gate in the Eastern Northeast is necessary to avoid any situation of the gate's being in a debilitated position. In figure 120, the gate is in front of the door. However, the gate is in a debilitated position, the Eastern Southeast. Therefore another gate must be placed in the Northern Northeast.

In houses facing North (fig. 121), if a gate in front of the main door falls into the debilitated position of the Northern Northwest, it should be corrected with a gate in the Northern Northeast.

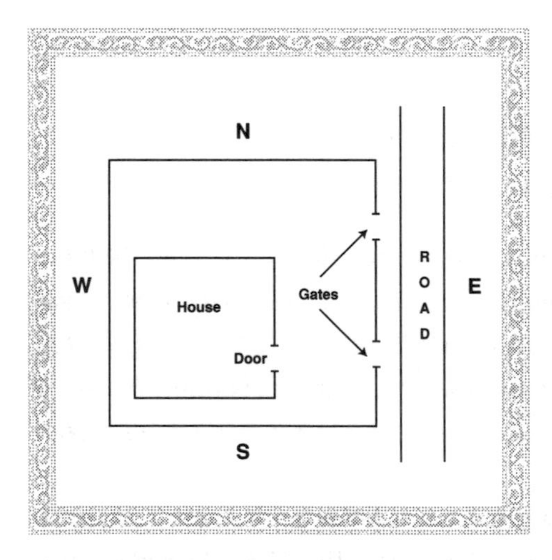

Fig. 120: Correction of defective gate in Eastern Southeast

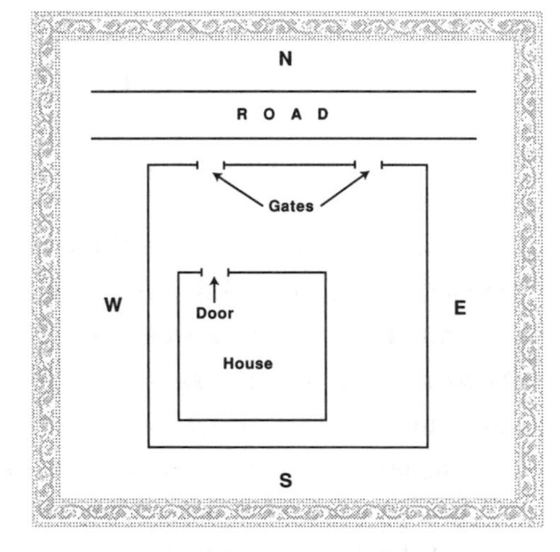

Fig. 121: The front gate in front of the main door is slightly toward Northern Northwest

In the case of a house facing the West and a gate in front of the main door (fig. 122), another gate in the Western Northwest is necessary.

If the house faces South, a gate in the Southern Southeast is necessary in addition to the gate in front of the door, as shown in figure 123.

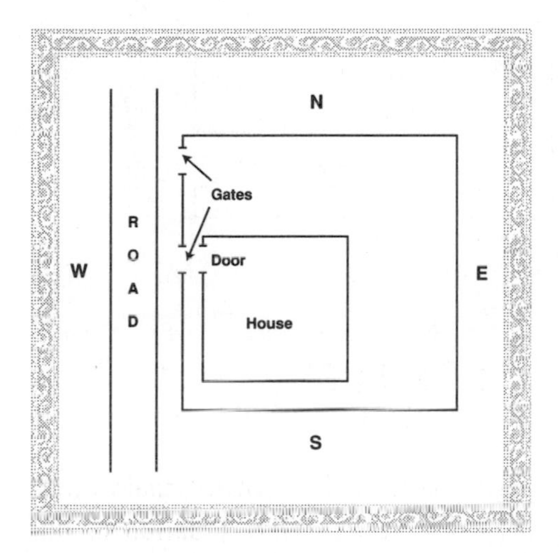

Fig. 122: Correction for a West-facing house

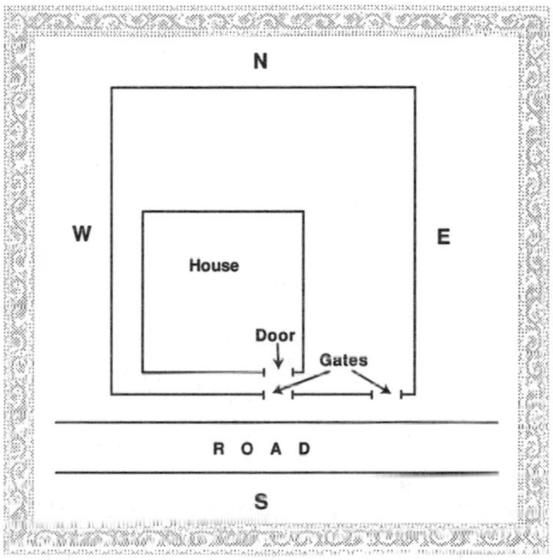

Fig. 123: Correction for a South-facing house

When a house faces the South or the West and has a single gate in an exalted position, a second gate is not necessary. However, a small gate facing the front door is necessary for houses facing North or East.

PLACEMENT OF MAIN DOOR FOR A BUILDING ON AN INCLINED PLOT

Even though a plot is inclined, the foundation must be parallel to the boundaries of the plot. Vaastu dictates that the front door should be placed toward the road. However, that can result in defects such as those shown in figures 124–29. Figure 124 shows a house with a door in the Eastern Northeast and an inclination toward a debilitated position, which is the Eastern Southeast. To correct this defect a door must be placed in the Northern Northeast.

In a plot with a Southern Southeast extension, a defect is created if the main door of the house faces toward the Southern Southwest (fig. 125). To correct this defect a door must be placed in the Northern Northeast.

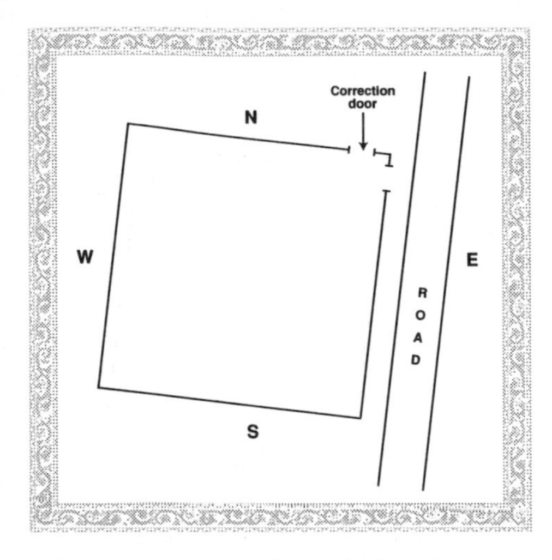

Fig. 124: Correction for an inclined house facing East

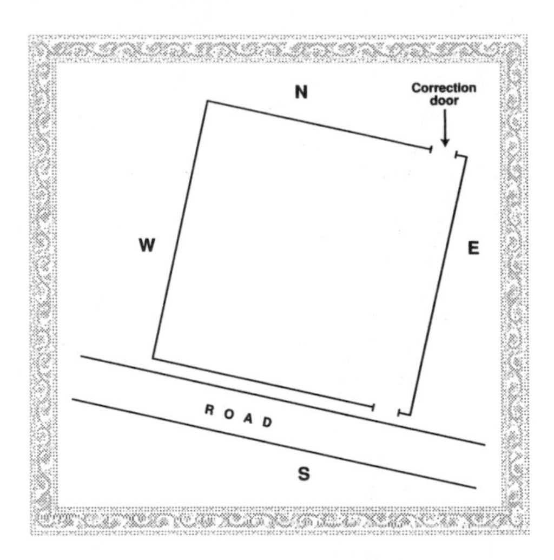

Fig. 125: Correction for an inclined house with front door facing toward Southern Southwest

The plot in figure 126 has a Southern Southwest extension. The main door in the Southern Southeast faces slightly toward the Southern Southeast. However, the Southern Southeast and Western Northwest cannot have any inclination. Hence, a correction door must be placed in the Eastern Northeast.

Figure 127 shows a plot with a Western Southwest extension. A main door in the Western Northwest faces the Western Northwest with an inclination. Hence, another door must be placed in the Northern Northeast to correct this defect.

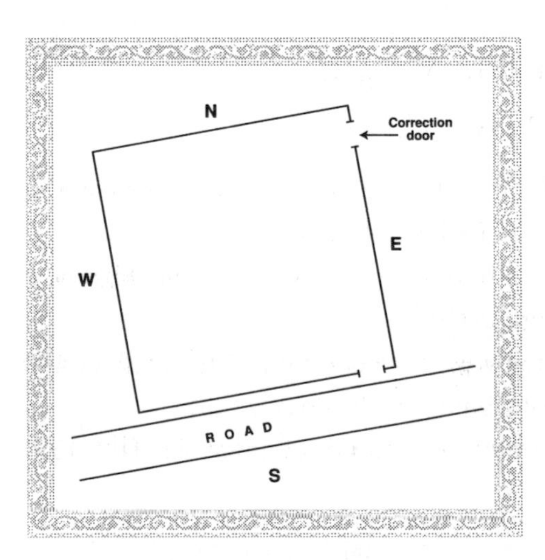

Fig. 126: Correction for front door facing toward Southern Southeast

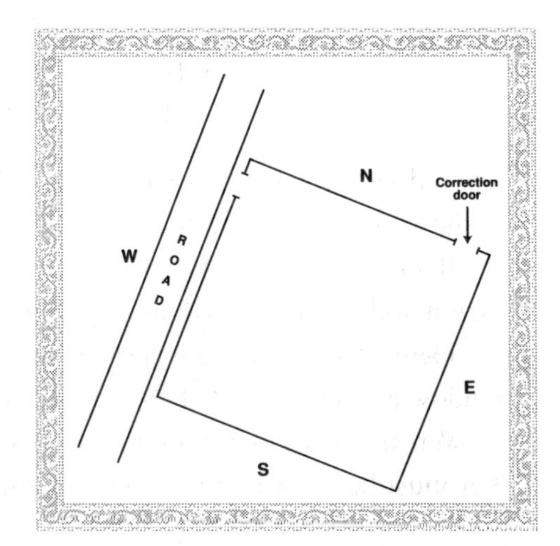

Fig. 127: Correction door for an inclined house facing West with a Western Southwest extension

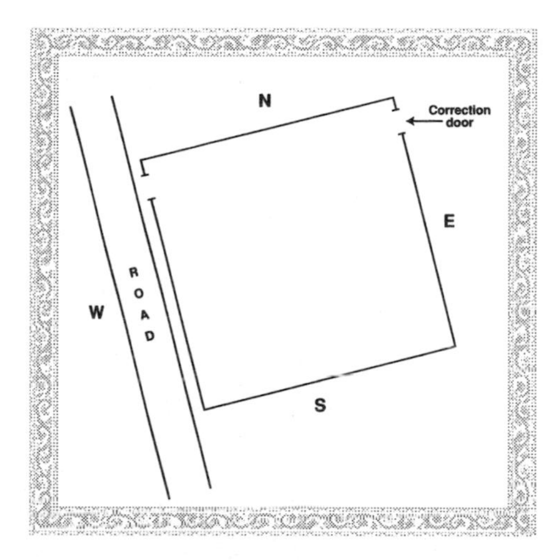

Fig. 128: Correction door for an inclined house facing West with Western Northwest extension

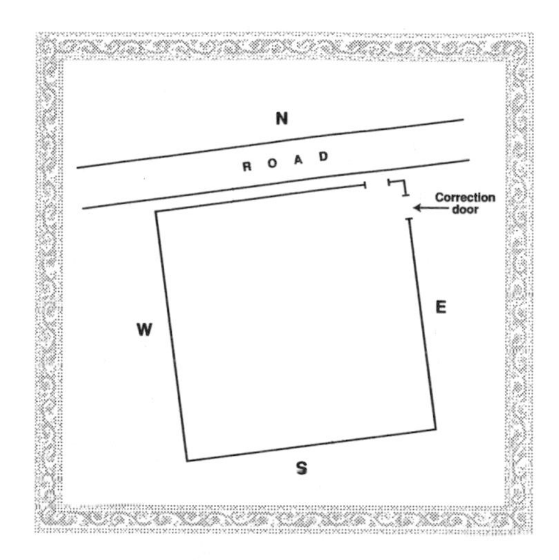

Fig. 129: Correction door for a North-facing house

Figure 128 shows a plot with a Western Northwest extension. A door in the Western Northwest faces the Western Southwest. To correct this defect a door must be placed in the Eastern Northeast.

Figure 129 shows a plot with a Northern Northeast extension. A main door in the Northern Northeast faces the Northern Northwest. Hence, another door must be placed in the Eastern Northeast to correct this defect.

ALIGNMENT OF DOORS, GATES, AND WINDOWS

When doors, windows, or gates face each other, their midpoints should be aligned, as shown in figure 130, in order to prevent blocking of energy flow.

If facing doors and windows are of different sizes, the midpoint alignment should still be maintained, as shown in figure 131.

Figure 132 shows an incorrect situation where the central points of a door and window are not aligned. This causes a disturbance in the energy flow.

When two windows are facing each other and are not of equal size (fig. 133) they must be aligned at least on one side.

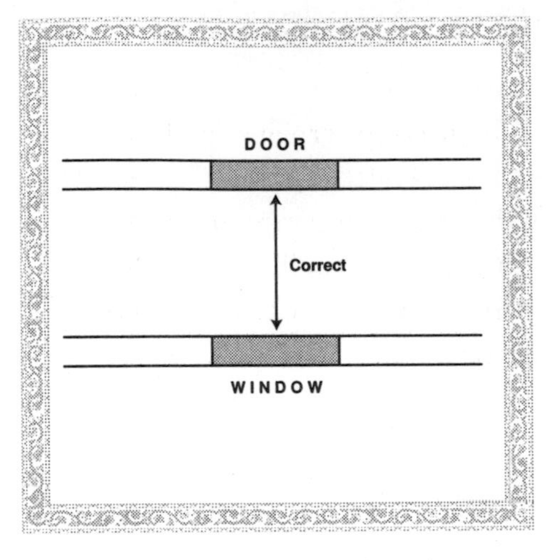

Fig. 130: Correct door and window positions

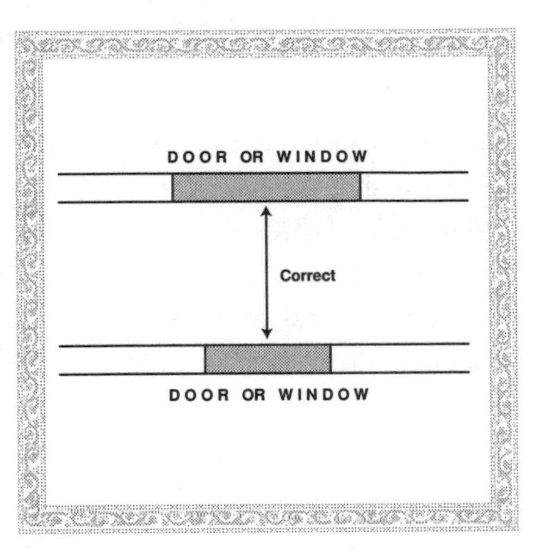

Fig. 131: Correct alignment of windows and doors of different sizes

Fig. 132: Incorrect alignment of doors and windows

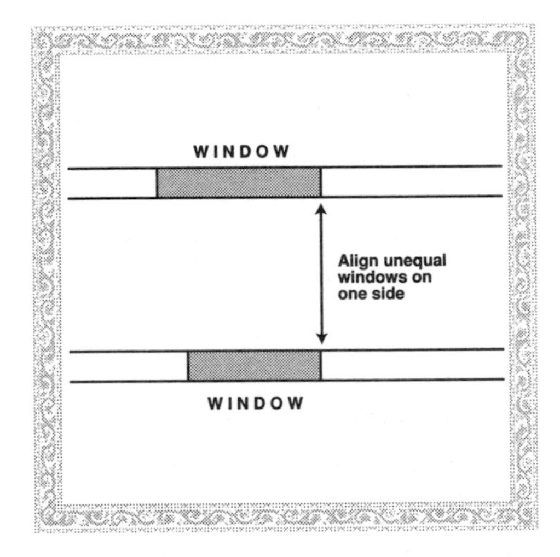

Fig. 133: Correct alignment of windows of unequal sizes

SHUTTERS AND BLOCKAGES

When there are double shutters on the roadside, the one on the exalted side should not be closed and the one on the debilitated side should not be kept open. It is good vaastu if both shutters are open or if the one on the exalted side is open and the one on the debilitated side is closed.

Another inauspicious feature in vaastu is having a pillar, tree, or a column in front of a door. This brings life-threatening consequences.

MOVEMENT WITHIN A BUILDING

Once you enter a building, the movement should be toward the exalted position. This may cause confusion if not understood properly. After entering through the door one should not straightaway move toward a debilitated position. After taking a minimum of three steps toward an exalted direction, movement may be changed that could be toward a debilitated position. This principle applies to moving within both a house and an individual room. In figure 134 the short arrows indicate the minimum three steps toward the exalted position.

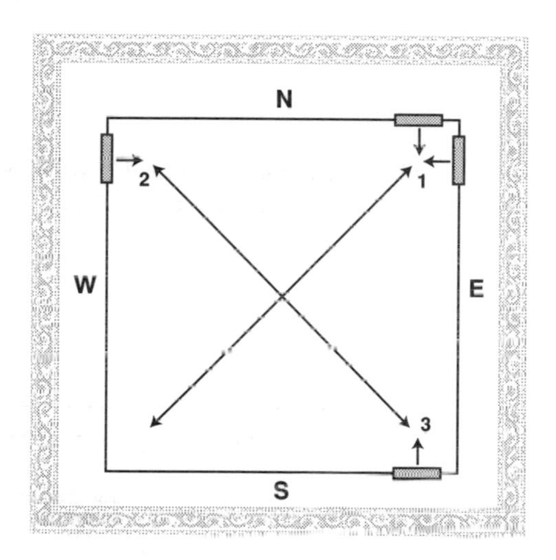

Fig. 134: Correct movement within a building

The situation numbered "1" in figure 134 shows the entrance from the Northeast and subsequent movement toward the Southwest. After entering the building, one should take a few steps toward the exalted position. If the entry is from the Northern Northeast, movement should be toward the Southern Southeast, or if entry is from the Eastern Northeast, the movement should be toward the Northern Northwest. Similarly, if the entrance is from the Western Northwest (number 2) the movement should be first toward the Eastern Northeast. If the entrance is from the Southern Southeast (number 3) movement should be first toward the Northern Northeast.

Movement between Northeast and Southwest is called *Devayaana,* which literally means "the way of the angels." In other words it is the spiritual path that elevates a person to the final goal of enlightenment. One of the two planets that govern the Northeast, Ketu, is known as *mokshakaraka,* meaning "deliverer of enlightenment." The other planet, Jupiter, also known as Guru, gives spiritual knowledge. The planet that governs the Southwest, Rahu, is a like a postman, the one responsible for final delivery of truth. Therefore, a movement from the Northeast constitutes a movement with full knowledge and wisdom of truth toward the Southwest, to finally be blessed with self-realization.

The movement from the Northwest to the Southeast is called *Pitruyaana,* meaning “the way of the *pitrus*” (forefathers or departed souls). It signifies worldly life, getting caught in the cycles of birth and death. If the house is built in accordance with vaastu science, one is expected to possess and enjoy worldly comforts to the fullest extent and still have the knowledge and wisdom to realize the ultimate truth and free oneself from worldly bondage and the cycle of birth and death.

CHAPTER 23

VAASTU FOR APARTMENTS AND COMMERCIAL BUILDINGS

APARTMENTS

In apartment complexes the vaastu of the unit itself has the greatest effect on the occupants. An apartment unit should be arranged according to the principles previously described to provide good vaastu in the Northeast sector. Ground level units bring more positive results than upper level units. However, the vaastu of the whole complex does have some effect on all of the occupants. Apartments located in the Northeast sector of the complex will provide better vaastu results.

COMMERCIAL BUILDINGS

If the building faces a road to the East, the cashier should sit in the Southeast sector and face either the North or the East (fig. 135). While facing the East, the cash register should be to the right side and while facing the North, to the left side.

If the building faces a road to the North (fig. 136), the cashier should sit in the Northwest corner facing the North or the East, and the cash register should be on the South side in case of the East facing and the West side in case of the North facing.

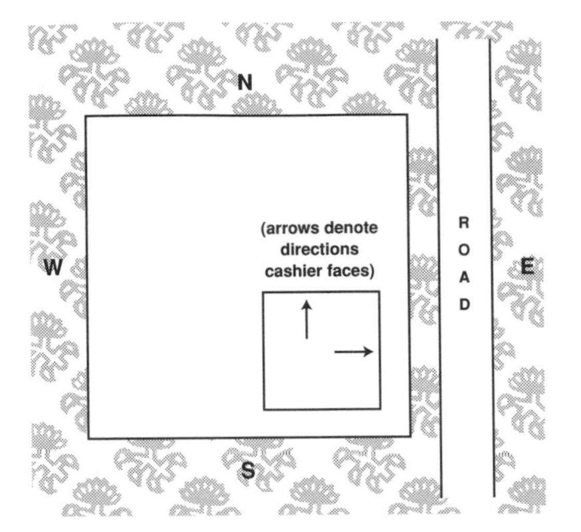

Fig. 135: East-facing shop and cashier's position

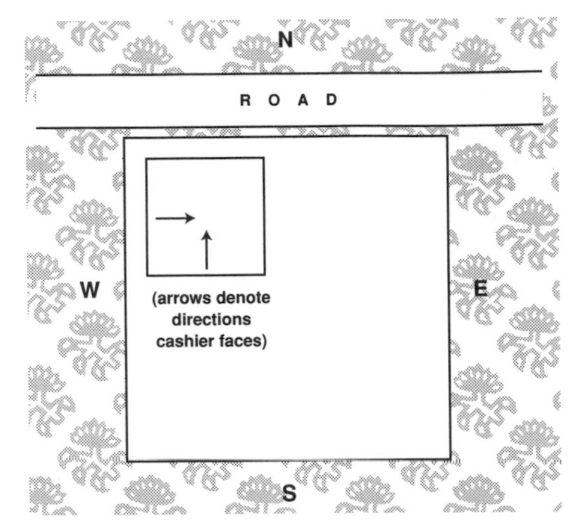

Fig. 136: North-facing shop and cashier's position

If the building faces a road to the West (fig. 137), the cashier should sit in the Southwest corner facing the North or the East, and the cash register should be on either the West or the South side.

If the building faces a road to the South (fig. 138), the cashier should sit in the Southwest corner facing the North or the East, and the cash register should be to the West or the South.

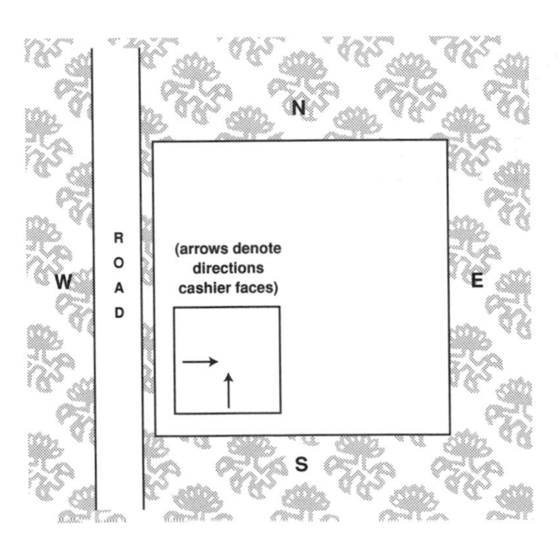

Fig. 137: West-facing shop and cashier's position

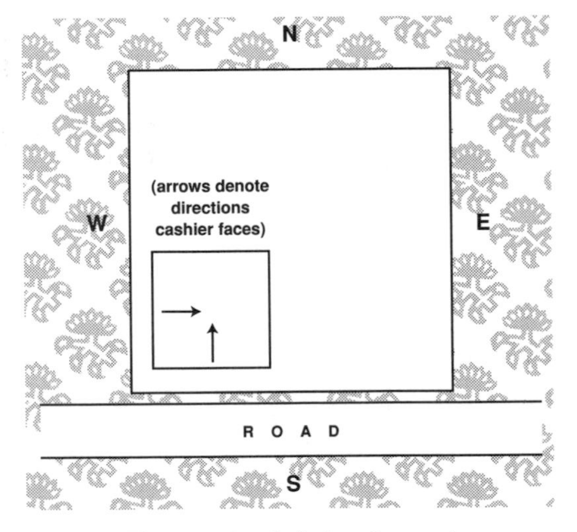

Fig. 138: South-facing shop and cashier's position

PART FIVE

VAASTU IN PRACTICE

CHAPTER 24

VAASTU CONSULTATION

A VAASTU CONSULTANT SHOULD BE ABLE to consult on property, existing buildings, new construction, interior design and decoration, and landscaping. A consultant can provide valuable guidance for owners, architects, contractors, and interior designers. Ancient vaastu texts describe the required qualifications for a vaastu consultant as follows: "A vaastu *Vidwan* (one who is learned in vaastu) should be well versed in various arts and have knowledge of astrology, astronomy, medicine, mathematics, architecture, gems, interior design, and construction." The ancient vedic culture was quite knowledgeable in these subjects, and the Indus Valley civilization was one of the most advanced civilizations on earth. Their understanding of nature and its intricate balance was deep and extensive, allowing them to live in much greater harmony than we do today.

In our present-day search for greater well-being in life, various alternative and complementary medicines such as ayurveda are becoming part of mainstream medicine. This has evoked interest in the knowledge and application of other vedic sciences, including vaastu. In my practice I have helped several families who were suffering from various chronic health ailments or financial problems. After following my suggestions and correcting their vaastu, these families are now enjoying better health and prosperity, and it has been very satisfying to see the smiles on their faces.

By applying the detailed information given in this book, you will be able to assess most common vaastu situations. Whether you are purchasing property, planning construction of a home or other building, or seeking rectification for an existing building, most of the necessary information is given here. In the next chapter I have summarized all of the considerations mentioned in Parts III and IV in the form of a scoring methodology that you can use to assess the suitability of a piece of property, proposed design, or existing house. However, in more complex situations, especially in doing rectifications for existing properties, you may need further assistance from a vaastu expert.

In a majority of cases, small corrections such as rearranging furniture, coordinating colors, or changing a few windows and doors will do the magic. Many extensions and cuts can be easily rectified by small changes to the property, such as the one I suggested to clients whose property had a Southern Southwest extension (fig. 139). Following my recommendation, they constructed a patio on the Southeast side to correct the defect (fig. 140).

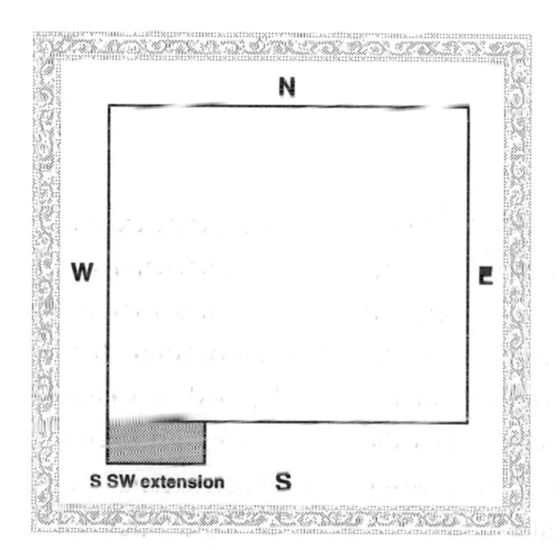

Fig. 139: Property with Southern Southwest extension

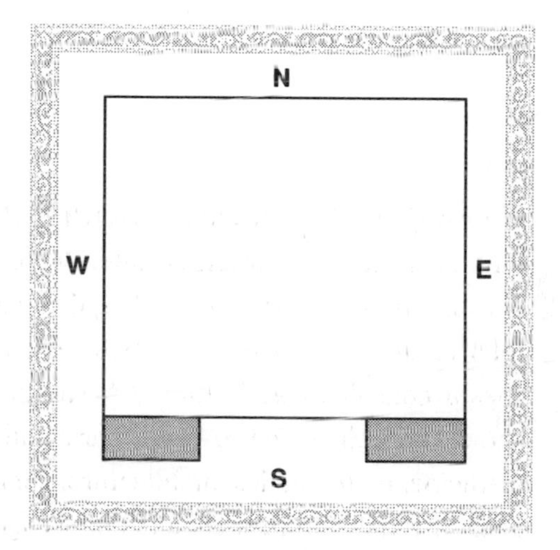

Fig. 140: Small patio added on the Southeast side as correction

In another case, I did a vaastu consultation for a family consisting of a father and two sons. The father was retired and his elder son was a stockbroker who had been working very hard. In two years he had been able to build a small portfolio of four million dollars for his clients. The second son was an unemployed college dropout—a source of agony for the father and older brother. The house they were renting had a complete block in the Northeast, and the entrance to the apartment was in the Western Southwest. The kitchen and a toilet were in the Northeast. All

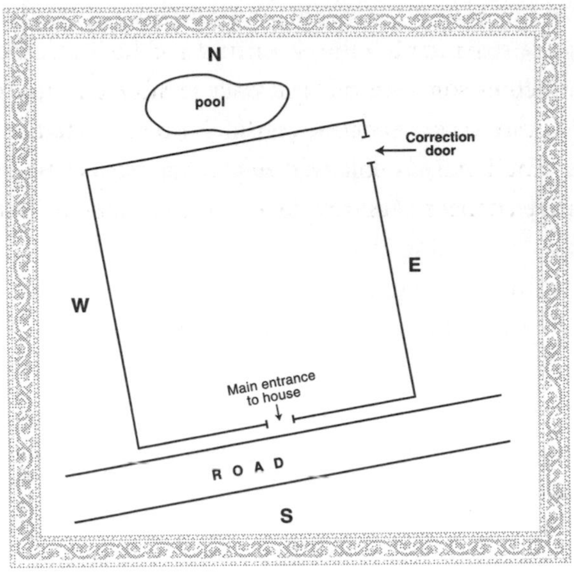

Fig. 141: House with a 20-degree Northern Northeast extension

these defects contributed to the family's lack of financial and educational progress.

They consulted me about buying the house shown in figure 141. It had a Northeast master bedroom upstairs and a basement underneath the entire house. It also had a swimming pool in the backyard to the North. The fireplace was in the Eastern Northeast of the family room. I noted that the house had several good vaastu features—such as the pool to the North, which brings great prosperity. I suggested that they buy the house and make some corrections.

The main door of the house was in the South, slightly off the midpoint toward the West. At first it appeared that the house had a Southern Southwest door—on to a debilitated position—but the front door was acceptable because the property extended by 20 degrees in the North, causing the main door to face toward the Southern Southeast—an exalted position. However, to address the problems of the second son, I suggested that they increase the positive energy by adding a correction door in the Eastern Northeast. I also told them that they should not use the fireplace because its location in the Northeast would cause financial and other difficulties, especially to male children.

In addition, I recommended that the father stay in the upstairs master bedroom, the second son stay in the basement bedroom in the Northwest, and a room be built for the elder son in the basement in the Southwest. That location was good for the elder son, as he was the main wage earner of the family. There was enough sunlight coming through two windows near the ceiling, and the room could be easily and simply built. The Northeast bedroom upstairs was acceptable because there was a family room and vacant space underneath it in the basement.

These changes were made to the house and the family moved in. Within one year, the elder son's business thrived and he built a portfolio of sixty million dollars. The second son reenrolled in college after ten months of living in the new house and began to get very good grades. He also started an internet business that is doing well. The family is enjoying all-around prosperity and is totally ecstatic about the positive changes that have taken place in such a short period of time.

CHAPTER 25

VAASTU ASSESSMENT OF BUILDINGS AND PROPERTY

IN ORDER TO SIMPLIFY THE APPLICATION of the several vaastu tenets presented in the previous chapters, I have summarized them in a comprehensive scoring methodology. Below you will find two separate Score Sheets, the first for the assessment of a building and property together (pages 120–24), and the second for the assessment of land only (pages 125–26).

Circle the most appropriate answer to the questions that follow. Answer only the questions that are applicable to your situation.

HOW TO CALCULATE THE RESULTS OF YOUR ANSWERS

Definitions:

Minimum Vaastu Score (MVS) = 3 × number of questions answered

Property (Residential or Land) Vaastu Score (PVS) = sum total of all points of your answers

Optimum Vaastu Score (OVS) = 5 × number of questions answered

Vaastu Percentage Score (VPS) = (PVS divided by OVS) × 100

Sample Calculation:

MVS = 10 questions were answered = 10 × 3 = 30
PVS = Total sum of answers = 40
OVS = 10 questions were answered = 10 × 5 = 50
VPS = 40 (PVS) divided by 50 (OVS) × 100 = 80%

Results:

1. If PVS is equal to or greater than MVS, then you are living in an acceptable vaastu home.
2. If PVS is less than MVS, then it is an unacceptable vaastu and rectification is needed.
3. Ideally, one should strive for a VPS of 75% or greater to truly enjoy the vaastu benefits.

SCORE SHEET A:
Assessment of Building and Property

QUESTION NUMBER	WHERE OR HOW ARE THE FOLLOWING LOCATED?	1 POINT	2 POINTS	3 POINTS	4 POINTS	5 POINTS
1	Kitchen	NE		Center N Center E	NW SW Center W Center S	SE
2	Master Bedroom	NE		SE NW		SW
3	Bathroom / Toilets	NE		SW		SE NW S W
4	Staircase	NE	Center N Center E			NW SE S W
5	Staircase Direction		Counterclockwise, South to North West to East			Clockwise North to South East to West
6	Bramhastana (center of the house)	Kitchen Body of Water Toilet Bedroom				Skylight Open to sky
7	Front Entrance Door	SSW WSW NNW ESE			Center N Center E Center W Center S	NNE ENE SSE WNW

QUESTION NUMBER	WHERE OR HOW ARE THE FOLLOWING LOCATED?	1 POINT	2 POINTS	3 POINTS	4 POINTS	5 POINTS
8	Well, Pond, or Lake	W S SE NW			Center North Center East	NE
9	Septic Tank	S W		ESE NNW NNE ENE		Mid East Mid North
10	Basement/ Cellar	SW SE NW Any combination				• NE • Whole basement • NE & NW • NE, NW & SE
11	Floor Levels—inside the house		• NE higher than NW or SE or SW • SW lower than SE or NW or NE • NW higher than SW or SE • NW lower than NE • SE higher than SW • SE lower than NW or NE			• All one level • NE lower than NW or SE or SW • SW higher than SE or NW or NE • NW lower than SW or SE • NW higher than NE • SE lower than SW • SE higher than NW or NE

SCORE SHEET A:
Assessment of Building and Property (continued)

QUESTION NUMBER	WHERE OR HOW ARE THE FOLLOWING LOCATED?	1 POINT	2 POINTS	3 POINTS	4 POINTS	5 POINTS
12	Floor Levels—level of plot		• NE higher than NW or SE or SW • SW lower than SE or NW or NE • NW higher than SW or SE • NW lower than NE • SE higher than SW • SE lower than NW or NE			• All one level • NE lower than NW or SE or SW • SW higher than SE or NW or NE • NW lower than SW or SE • NW higher than NE • SE lower than SW • SE higher than NW or NE
13	Roof Level		• NE higher than NW or SE or SW • SW lower than SE or NW or NE • NW higher than SW or SE • NW lower than NE • SE higher than SW • SE lower than NW or NE			• All one level • NE lower than NW or SE or SW • SW higher than SE or NW or NE • NW lower than SW or SE • NW higher than NE • SE lower than SW • SE higher than NW or NE

QUESTION NUMBER	WHERE OR HOW ARE THE FOLLOWING LOCATED?	1 POINT	2 POINTS	3 POINTS	4 POINTS	5 POINTS
14	Compound Wall		N higher than S E higher than W	No compound wall		All four sides one level S higher than N W higher than E
15	Front Gate	NNW SSW WSW ESE			Center E Center N Center W Center S	ENE NNE WNW SSE
16	Space between house perimeter and plot perimeter—East-West orientation	W>E			E=W	E>W
17	Space between house perimeter and plot perimeter—North-South orientation	S>N			N=S	N>S
18	House Cuts	NE		SW SE NW		No cuts
19	House Extensions	SW	NW SE			NE
20	Neighboring Houses		• House on E or N is higher or equal; No compound wall is on E or N • No houses on S or W but house exists on N or E or both	• House on E or N higher, and your property has a compound wall	• Houses are of equal heights on all sides • No houses	• Houses on W, S higher • Houses on N, E lower

SCORE SHEET A:
Assessment of Building and Property (continued)

QUESTION NUMBER	WHERE OR HOW ARE THE FOLLOWING LOCATED?	1 POINT	2 POINTS	3 POINTS	4 POINTS	5 POINTS
21	Directions of water flow (from stream, river)	• E to W on South side • N to S on West side		• W to E on South side • S to N on West side	• E to W on North side • N to S on East side	• W to E on North side • S to N on East side
22	Road Focus	NNW WSW SSW ESE		Center N Center S Center W Center E		NNE ENE SSE WNW
23	Convergent structure (U-shaped) open toward:	S W				N E
24	Divergent structure (L-shaped) open toward:	SE SW NW				NE
25	Road on North side	Above plot level	Below plot level and sloping to West	Above plot level and sloping to East	At plot level	Below plot level and/or sloping to East
26	Road on East side	Above plot level	Below plot level and sloping to South	Above plot level and sloping to North	At plot level	Below plot level and/or sloping to North
27	Road on West side	Below plot level and sloping to South	Below plot level	Below plot level and sloping to North	At plot level	Above plot level and/or sloping to North
28	Road on South side	Below plot level and sloping to West	Below plot level	Below plot level and sloping to East	At plot level	Above plot level and/or sloping to East

SCORE SHEET B:
Assessment of Land Only

QUESTION NUMBER	WHERE OR HOW ARE THE FOLLOWING LOCATED?	1 POINT	2 POINTS	3 POINTS	4 POINTS	5 POINTS
1	Road on North side	Above plot level			At plot level	Below plot level
2	Road on East side	Above plot level			At plot level	Below plot level
3	Road on West side	Below plot level			At plot level	Above plot level
4	Road on South side	Below plot level			At plot level	Above plot level
5	Road focus	NNW ESE SSW WSW	Center S Center W		Center E Center N	NNE ENE WNW ESE
6	Position of the plot —in relation to other plots	Small plot sandwiched between two large plots				
7	Ponds, Lakes, Wells, and Water Streams	S W SW	NW SE		N E	NE
8	Tall structures around land (like buildings, mountains, hills)	E N NE				W S SW
9	Other considerations	Plots situated near cemeteries				

SCORE SHEET B:
Assessment of Land Only (continued)

QUESTION NUMBER	WHERE OR HOW ARE THE FOLLOWING LOCATED?	1 POINT	2 POINTS	3 POINTS	4 POINTS	5 POINTS
10	Land sloping down	W S SW			Flat land	E N NE
11	Directions of water flow (from stream, river)	• E to W on South side • N to S on West side		• W to E on South side • S to N on West side	• E to W on North side; • N to S on East side	• W to E on North side • S to N on East side
12	Extensions	WSW SSW		WNW NNW ESE SSE		• all 4 corners 90 degrees • NE extended
13	Cuts	NE			SSW WSW ESE SSE NNW WNW	
14	Shape	Triangular Circular Irregular Many angles			Triangular with N or E extension	Square Rectangular

CHAPTER 26

VAASTU AND FENG SHUI

VAASTU AND THE CHINESE ART OF PLACEMENT, feng shui (pronounced "fung schway"), both date from antiquity and share certain characteristics. Both sciences have long histories. Vaastu dates back to the vedic period in India, around 5000–7000 B.C.E., while feng shui dates back to 1700 B.C.E. in China. Sages in both India and China went to great depths in search of the meaning of our existence on Earth and discovered very many hidden secrets. Both came to understand that everything in the whole universe is interconnected—not one single atom is truly separate and independent from the others.

Feng shui—meaning wind and water—has been popular in China throughout its history, having been promoted by various dynasties. Several variations of feng shui are practiced in different parts of China today. The most popular form—mandarin feng shui—is now being practiced worldwide. Tibetans also practice a variant of feng shui that can also be seen as a form of Indian vaastu. Although over the millennia the practices of feng shui and vaastu have diverged, both are based on astrological considerations and elemental influences. There are many similarities in the two astrological traditions, which appear to have a common origin in ancient vedic astrology. The house of nine palaces referred to in feng shui corresponds to the solar yantra of vedic astrology. The concept of exalted and debilitated positions that is fundamental to vaastu is based on the energy flow between the nine planets, while in feng shui it is said that if you understand Pa-K'ua (energy) and the nine palaces, "you will uncover the mystery of the universe."

Like feng shui, vaastu sees the planetary forces as the determining factors in the distribution of energy (chi). Based on this principle of the distribution of energy, vaastu has formulated certain basic principles that are constant, such as height and weight. Colors, textures, materials, and designs play a significant role in vaastu, based on the character of the governing planets and elements.

The overall characters of the planets and their various influences are very similar in vaastu and feng shui. However, there are some differences in the colors associated with the planets. For example, Indian astrology associates Saturn with the color blue, while Chinese astrology associates it with yellow and gold. These types of variations are common in any occult science because of differences in interpretations by the seers. To quote a vedic phrase, *ekamsat vipra bahudha vadanti:* "Truth is one but the sages explain it differently."

Using the theory of primordial elements to describe various subtle energies is common to both traditions. The Chinese describe the five basic elements as metal, wood, water, fire, and earth, while the Indian tradition considers wood and metal as part of earth and adds the elements of space and air. In vaastu these five elements are described as evolving one from the other. They are not only physical manifestations but also the subtle energy principles behind the elements. For example, ether represents pure space. That does not mean it is empty—it is full of matter in its first stage of creation from energy. Modern subatomic physics explains that matter and energy are interchangeable at this stage, depending on the observer's point of view. This phase is called ether.

When the ether element starts moving with intense speed, it becomes the moving principle of air. This is how physics explains the formation of new stars in the billions of galaxies in the universe. When the air principle intensifies, heat is generated. The intense speed of the particles creates heat. This is how one sees the glowing stars and planets. Physics describes this as hydrogen gas. When hydrogen is burnt, it combines with oxygen atoms and forms water. Vedic seers seem to have understood the concept of water being generated from fire even before modern physicists explained this phenomenon. When the water element cools, it solidifies and the solidification is known as the earth principle.

According to the vedic understanding, the entire universe from atoms to stars is sustained and governed by these five elements. Although the Chinese describe the elements differently, understanding this principle intuitively and applying it with common sense is key to both vaastu and feng shui.

Feng shui considers two kinds of chi (energy)—yin (dark, receptive) and yang (bright, creative)—and talks about aligning with the geomagnetism of Earth. It considers the door position as North and uses that as a reference point for assessing the chi distribution in order to arrange interiors. Vaastu, on the other hand, begins with North as indicated by a magnetic compass. Before the invention of the magnetic compass, perfect North was determined using methods based on the position of the sun. All of the other directions are derived from the North as the reference point.

Vaastu has a strong core of mathematics and a detailed measuring system, making it more objective and consistent with vedic astrology than feng shui. Lacking a similar depth of measurements and calculations, feng shui is more arbitrary, subjective, and esoteric. One aspect of feng shui—the feng shui of yin domain—is used for the selection of burial sites, while another aspect—the feng shui of the yang domain—deals with residences and businesses. Unlike vaastu, feng shui considers many shapes of land and water bodies and correlates these with various animals.

Two subjects, two origins, two approaches, two logistics—they each succeed in achieving what they individually set out to do. Feng shui offers simple solutions to correct defects such as placing a mirror, hanging a picture or a plant, changing the color of a wall, and so on. However, because of its mathematical approach, vaastu often recommends more drastic corrections, such as tearing down a wall or moving a door. Feng shui opens the Pandora's box and hands you the "cures." Vaastu makes sure you do not open the box at all. Feng shui is the hospital; vaastu is the health club.

APPENDIX

ANCIENT VAASTU TEXTS

1. *Viswakarma Prakash* and *Vaastupadavinyas*—deal with statues, residences, and palaces.
2. The following Puranas describe the vaastu of residential buildings, temples, town planning, carvings, banquet halls, pillars, and plantations: *Agnipurana, Vayupurana, Skandapurana, Garudapuvana, Matsyapurana,* and *Suryapurana.*
3. *Brihat Samhita*—deals with surveying, plantations, and residential and temple architecture.
4. *Manasara*—discusses the universality of vaastu tradition and also contains iconography of Jain and Buddhist images.
5. *Brihat Jatak*—describes qualifications for a vaastu specialist.
6. *Mayamatam*—deals extensively with the vaastu of dwelling sites, discussing soil, measurement, orientation, villages, towns, and temples. The text discusses the importance of doors, gateways, pavilions, vehicles, beds, and seats. Maya, the author, was also known to have been an expert in astrology. This is the best treatise on vaastu known to have originated from South India.
7. *Viswakarma Vaastushastra*—known to be a great vaastu treatise of the sixth century C.E., this treatise addresses the sites and materials to be used in vaastu construction. It examines soil, town and village planning,

the construction of temples, palaces, mansions, inner royal courts, and dining halls.

8. *Samarangana Sutradhara*—this Buddhist work discusses building construction on the basis of vaastu. Lord Buddha is said to have delivered discourses on architecture and even told his disciples that supervising the construction of a building was one of the duties of the order.
9. The following *agamas*—works describing the techniques of worship—address the architecture of temples: *Kamikagama, Karanagama, Suprabhedagama,* and *Vaikhanasagama.*
10. The following tantra works also contain information on vaastu: *Kirana Tantra, Hayasheesha Tantra,* and *Kautilya Arthashastra.*

APPENDIX B

VITAL DIMENSION (*AYAM*)

THE VITAL DIMENSION OR *AYAM* is a measurement of the outer foundation area of a structure, calculated by multiplying length times breadth times 9 and dividing by 8 (length times breadth times 9/8). The resultant remainder determines the *ayam* to which each structure belongs. Each *ayam* has particular effects, as shown in the chart below. Although it is discussed in detail in many ancient vaastu texts, it is considered by most modern vaastu experts—including my teacher—to be more important for royal mansions than for modern-day homes. The details of the *ayam* are given below for information purposes only.

REMAINDER	AYAM	EFFECT
1	*Dhwajaayam*: Sovereign dimension	Financial fortune
2	*Dhumaayam*: Smoke dimension	Ill health to heads of family
3	*Simhaayam*: Lion dimension	Health, wealth, prosperity, powerful victory
4	*Shwanaayam*: Dog dimension	Ill health
5	*Vrishabhaayam*: Taurus dimension	Financial fortune
6	*Kharaayam*: Donkey dimension	Nomadic life and bad luck
7	*Gajaayam*: Elephant dimension	Health and wealth
8	*Kaakaayam:* Crow dimension	Sorrow and shattered life

APPENDIX C

VAASTU AT A GLANCE

The chart that follows offers a brief outline of the ideal vaastu of a residence. The columns indicate the cardinal directions and Brahmasthana; the rows indicate the different features of a home and the factors that can influence positive or negative vaastu. Using this chart, it is possible to quickly review your existing home on its vaastu merits and plan for future residences.

	N	E	S	W	SW	SE	NW	NE
Height	Lower than South or equal	Lower than West or equal	Higher than North or equal	Higher than East or equal	Highest height	Lower than SW, higher than NW and NE	Lower than SW, SE, higher than NE	Lowest, should not be higher than SW, SE, NW
Weight					Maximum weight	SW, heavier than NW and NE	SW, SE, heavier than NE	Should not be heavier than SW, SE, NW
Extensions				Unacceptable	Unacceptable	Unacceptable	Unacceptable	Acceptable—ideal
Cuts					Acceptable	Acceptable	Acceptable	Unacceptable
Land, floor, roof	Lower than South or equal	Lower than West or equal	Higher than North or equal	Higher than East or equal	Equal in height and weight or greater than SE, NW, and NE	Equal in height and weight or lesser than SW, and higher than NW and NE	Equal in height and weight or lesser than SW and SE or greater than NE	Equal or lesser than SW, SE, and NW
Sloping down to	N = S or N lower than S	E = W or E lower than W	S to N	W to E				
Exalted and Debilitated (Ex and De)								
Master bedroom					First preference	Second preference	Third preference	Not recommended
Daughter's room		East of master bedroom	On the South side			Either in SE or between SW and SE		
Son's room	North of master bedroom			On the West side		Either in NW or between SW and NW		
Guest room			Acceptable	Acceptable		Second preference	First preference	No bedrooms recommended
Kitchen			Acceptable	Acceptable	Third preference	First preference	Second preference	Never
Prayer room	Acceptable	Acceptable	Acceptable	Acceptable				First preference
Living room	Acceptable	Acceptable					Second preference	First preference
Family room	Acceptable	Acceptable					Second preference	First preference

	NNE	ENE	ESE	SSE	SSW	WSW	WNW	NNW	BRAHMASTHANA
Height									
Weight									
Extensions	Acceptable	Acceptable	Unacceptable	Unacceptable	Unacceptable	Unacceptable	Unacceptable	Unacceptable	
Cuts	Unacceptable	Unacceptable	Acceptable	Acceptable	Acceptable	Acceptable	Acceptable	Acceptable	
Land, floor, roof									
Sloping down to									
Exalted and Debilitated (Ex and De)	Ex	Ex	De	Ex	De	De	Ex	De	
Master bedroom									
Daughter's room									
Son' room									
Guest room									
Kitchen									
Prayer room									First preference
Living room									
Family room									

	N	E	S	W	SW	SE	NW	NE
Library	Acceptable	Acceptable	Acceptable	Acceptable	Acceptable	Third preference	Second preference	First preference
Store			Acceptable	Acceptable	Acceptable	Acceptable	Acceptable	Unacceptable
Play and exercise	Acceptable	Acceptable	Preferred	Acceptable	Acceptable	Preferred	Acceptable	Acceptable but not heavy gym equipment
Bathroom	Acceptable	Acceptable	Acceptable	Acceptable	Acceptable except Eastern type squatting toilet in the SW corner	Acceptable	Acceptable	Unacceptable
1st child's position					SW sector			
2nd child's position						SE sector		
3rd child's position							NW sector	
4th—onward								NE sector
Staircase					Acceptable	Acceptable	Acceptable	Uncceptable
Male head				Governed by the West side				
Female head			Governed by the South side					
Female children	Governed by the North side							
Male children		Governed by the East side						
Animals							To be housed on the NW side	
Swings							Ideal location	
Well, pond, lake								To be in the NE sector

	NNE	ENE	ESE	SSE	SSW	WSW	WNW	NNW	BRAHMASTHANA
Library									
Store									
Play and exercise									
Bathroom									
1st child's position									
2nd child's position									
3rd child's position									
4th— onward									
Staircase									Uncceptable
Male head									
Female head									
Female children									
Male children									
Animals									
Swings									
Well, pond, lake									

	N	E	S	W	SW	SE	NW	NE
Over head water tank			Acceptable	Acceptable	To be in the SW corner			Never to be in the NE
Boilers (Water heaters) Meter board			Acceptable	Acceptable	Acceptable as a third preference	First preference	Acceptable as a second preference	Never to be in the NE
Heavy equipment	Unacceptable	Unacceptable	Good	Good	Preferred	Good	Acceptable	Unacceptable
Granary	Unacceptable	Unacceptable	Acceptable	Acceptable	Acceptable	Acceptable	First preference	Unacceptable
Computers			Acceptable	Acceptable	Third preference	First preference	Second preference	Unacceptable
AC Units			Acceptable	Acceptable	Third preference	First preference	Second preference	Unacceptable
Swimming pool								
Septic tank and chemical or any liquid storage	Central North	Central East						
Underground water storage								
Space around the house	Equal or greater than South	Equal or greater than West	Equal or lesser than North	Equal or lesser than East				
Land slope	Flat or sloping to North	Flat or sloping to East						
Front door								
Front gate								
Road focus								
INTERIOR DESIGN								
Colors	Emerald green, neutral shades of green,blue, gray, brown	Red, yellow, gold, orange	Red and fiery colors, jet black	Dark blue, brown, gray, black	Bright yellow, gold orange, transparent	Rainbowlike effect, pastels, light blues, pinks	White, light shades of, blue, green, pink	Yellow, orange, gold

	NNE	ENE	ESE	SSE	SSW	WSW	WNW	NNW	BRAHMASTHANA
Over head water tank									
Boilers (Water heaters) Meter board									Never to be in Brahmasthana
Heavy equipment									Unacceptable
Granary									Unacceptable
Computers									
AC units									
Swimming pool	Ideal location	Ideal location	Unacceptable	Unacceptable	Unacceptable	Unacceptable	Unacceptable	Unacceptable	Unacceptable
Septic tank and chemical or any liquid storage									
Underground water storage	Ideal location	Ideal location	Unacceptable	Unacceptable	Unacceptable	Unacceptable	Unacceptable	Unacceptable	Unacceptable
Space around the house									
Land slope									
Front door	Ideal	Ideal	Unacceptable	Ideal	Unacceptable	Unacceptable	Ideal	Unacceptable	
Front gate	Ideal	Ideal	Unacceptable	Ideal	Unacceptable	Unacceptable	Ideal	Unacceptable	
Road focus	Ideal	Ideal	Unacceptable	Ideal	Unacceptable	Unacceptable	Ideal	Unacceptable	
INTERIOR DESIGN									
Colors									

	N	E	S	W	SW	SE	NW	NE
Furniture					Heavy wood	Wrought iron and light wood	Light wood and rattan	Light rattan, light wood glass table top
Planets	Mercury	Sun	Mars	Saturn	Rahu	Venus	Moon	Jupiter, Ketu
Elements					Earth	Fire	Air	Water

	NNE	ENE	ESE	SSE	SSW	WSW	WNW	NNW	BRAHMASTHANA
Furniture									Avoid furniture
Planets									
Elements									Ether

BOOKS OF RELATED INTEREST

VAASTU: THE INDIAN ART OF PLACEMENT

Design and Decorate Homes to Reflect Eternal Spiritual Principles

by Rohit Arya

THE FENG SHUI COMPANION

A User-friendly Guide to the Ancient Art of Placement

by George Birdsall

FENG SHUI FOR LIFE

Mastering the Dynamics between Your Inner World and Outside Environment

by Jon Sandifer

TAOIST FENG SHUI

The Ancient Roots of the Chinese Art of Placement

by Susan Levitt

BEAUTY FENG SHUI

Chinese Techniques for Unveiling Your Inner Beauty

by Chao-Hsiu Chen

BODY FENG SHUI

The Ancient Chinese Science of Body Reading

by Chao-Hsiu Chen

SACRED GROUND TO SACRED SPACE

Visionary Ecology, Perennial Wisdom, Environmental Ritual and Art

by Rowena Pattee Kryder

Inner Traditions • Bear & Company

P.O. Box 388

Rochester, VT 05767

1-800-246-8648

www.InnerTraditions.com

Or contact your local bookseller